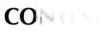

CONTINUOUS DEVELOPMENT

The
path
to
improved
performance

edited by
Sue Wood

Institute of Personnel Management

© Institute of Personnel Management 1988

First published 1988
Reprinted 1989 and 1990

Phototypeset by Illustrated Arts, Sutton, Surrey
and printed in Great Britain by Dotesios Printers Ltd.

British Library Cataloguing Publication Data
Continuous development.
  1. Personnel. Training – For management
  I. Wood, Sue
  658.3'124

ISBN 0-85292-405-4

Contents

Acknowledgements

The IPM is pleased to record its thanks to the Manpower Services Commission for providing the funds for the field research which allowed the IPM's National Committee for Training and Development to extend its original work in the field of continuous development and which underpins this book.

The case examples form the core of the book and the IPM is sincerely grateful to the many people, too many to name individually, who gave up their valuable time to discuss their organization's attitudes to and experiences of continuous development in practice. The case examples are particularly useful because the interviewees in each organization were willing to be frank and open with the IPM's research team. Not only were interviewees proud of their organization's success but they were also willing to share their experiences – good and bad – in order to help other people interested in introducing continuous development within their own organizations.

Lastly, the IPM acknowledges the research team which put this book together:

> Harry Barrington
> Dr Ron Johnson
> Keith Lathrope
> Professor Alan Mumford
> Sue Wood

All the authors contributed to all the chapters to a greater or lesser extent. However, the author(s) who made the primary contribution to each section are acknowledged in the chapter headings.

Chapter One
How to find your way around this book (and get the most from it)
Keith Lathrope and Sue Wood

Different readers of this book will have different reasons for reading it, and some readers will not wish to go through it from cover to cover.

For this reason, this chapter is a guide to the book, as the book itself is a guide to continuous development. Continuous development is an approach to promoting individual and organizational effectiveness and this book is for people who take seriously their responsibility for contributing to the success of business and other organizations.

This book is the result of the work of a team of people who have attempted to describe continuous development and set out the case for it. That team comprises: Harry Barrington, IPM's Chief Examiner (Employee Development), who spent 30 years with Lever Brothers Ltd's training departments; Dr Ron Johnson and Keith Lathrope, both now independent consultants with over 40 years' industrial and training experience between them; Professor Alan Mumford, who joined the academic fraternity after more than 20 years in industry and training; and Sue Wood, IPM's Manager – Training and Development.

You can use the book whether you are a manager, a personnel/training specialist or simply a learner wishing to take advantage of the opportunities that work itself provides for building further capabilities. Your own role and your own organization are unique of course, but the chapters are carefully written and the examples carefully chosen so that you should be able to relate them to your own situation:

1

For those who are unfamiliar with up to date methods of encouraging learning and improved performance, the book provides an introduction to the thinking and successful application from which continuous development (CD) derives, together with practical examples of the pay-offs which have been and can be achieved.

For those who are already closely involved with training and development, the book demonstrates the potential contribution of CD to the enhancement of current practice.

For those who wish to use the learning opportunities of their work to improve their capabilities, it focuses attention on what, realistically, can be achieved.

The scope of the book

Before you begin to formulate your reading plan, it might be helpful to ask yourself:

'What in particular, if anything, am I looking for?'
'How much do I already know about CD?'
'What might I be able to do if I discover something useful?'
'How much time have I, at present, to consider the contents of the book?'

Brief descriptions of each chapter are given below to help you 'tune in'.

Chapter Two: An introduction to continuous development

Because most people prefer to think about things before committing themselves, this chapter describes what is now generally regarded as being encompassed by 'continuous development'. It traces its evolution and explains the essential ideas and underlying concepts and the vital constituents which distinguish this approach to learning and improving performance. It also includes a section especially written for IPM students and a section on introducing CD within the organization.

Chapter Three: 'Continuous Development: People and Work': a code

The IPM's CD Code is reproduced in full. The Code was prepared for IPM members first but is intended for general distribution. It sets out guidelines for consideration and action. It demonstrates the need for the policies related to people management to incorporate specific commitment to CD. It details the responsibilities and roles of all who participate in the activity and provides guidance on how to recognize, create and exploit opportunities to promote CD. Perhaps most important of all, it confirms the advantages in performance which will be achieved.

Chapter Four: Case Examples

As one picture is worth a thousand words, so one case example is worth a thousand assertions. This assembly of case examples describes a variety of organizations, operating in very different circumstances, having very different aims and objectives, and faced with different challenges. What they have in common is a determination to develop and manage their people resource so as to 'grow the enterprise by growing the people'. How they have sought to do this varies from organization to organization. They started from different bases, they have encountered different problems and have reached different stages and experienced different successes.

What the examples are intended to demonstrate is that irrespective of the purposes of the organization and the services or products they provide to client or customer, a CD approach to enhancing the competence of the people working within them contributes significantly to success. The contribution does not depend upon size or scale, complexity or maturity, history or prospects. It does depend upon overcoming inertia, a resolution to succeed and persistence. The examples offer readers not only an opportunity to become aware of what others have been achieving but, more importantly, an opportunity to compare notes, take stock, think through the similarities and contrasts with your own organization and consider the implications. (You may prefer to begin by reading examples of organizations which have similarities to your own. If so, refer to the chart which appears at the beginning of the chapter.)

Chapter Five: Prompt lists

The value to be derived from reading accounts of other people's endeavours is not just restricted to acquiring aware-ness. It could and should be a springboard for action. The three Prompt Lists – for Personnel and Training Managers, Line Managers and for Senior Executives – are offered to help you to focus upon the key considerations for implement-ing CD within your organization. They are intended to help you to move from knowing more about the CD approach to formulating a plan of action to take advantage of it. CD involves everyone in the organization; however, a good start can be made in an individual unit of the organization. Whilst each Prompt List addresses the particular roles of particular readers, the lists interrelate. Other people have expectations of you, and the lists indicate what sort of co-operation you can expect from others. In providing your own answers to the questions in these Prompt Lists, you are creating a personal blueprint for action. You can also use a Prompt List as learning material for colleagues or subordinates by mak-ing it pre-meeting reading to go with an arranged item on an agenda. At the ensuing meeting, members' answers will show up the extent to which the team is committed to, and even the extent to which they agree about, continuous development.

Chapter Six: Enhancing your learning skills

Whatever encouragement is provided by the organization, in the last analysis the success of CD depends upon the learners' efforts. But not just effort. Much will depend upon their learning capabilities. There are learning skills and learning styles which vary from person to person. Identifying what these are, developing them further and applying them effectively will greatly assist the implementation of CD. This chapter provides practical help to those who want to get launched.

Setting an objective

Having read and reflected on the descriptions of the chapters, have your objectives in reading this book been clarified? Perhaps they are:

(1) A desire to keep up to date with what is happening in people management as it relates to organization performance. You need to know about CD.

(2) A requirement to find additional ways of building the competence of your workforce in order to raise your organization's performance. CD purports to be one way. You need to be able to judge its possible utility to your organization.

(3) An appreciation that your organization does not have all the answers. You are prepared to learn from others, and so you need to acquaint yourself with the experiences of others and to be able to judge their relevance and validity to your organization. You need to decide whether or not to implement an initiative.

(4) You are convinced already that CD makes sense. It is pertinent to your role and to your organization. You need to decide how to get started.

Of course, the hope is that if you start from any of the first three positions, the book will encourage you through to the fourth.

As you read through the material you will find it helpful to make a note of everything which guides your thinking towards your objective. Note in particular:

- that which is new to you in the thinking underlying CD
- those assertions and propositions which impress you as being defensible, and those which seem questionable
- those aspects of your knowledge and belief system which are confirmed, and those which are challenged
- any new insights you gain which might be worth considering more deeply.

From your notes, review the implications for you personally, for the contribution you are seeking to make to your organization, for others with whom you work, and for your organization as a whole. If you set out with objective (3) or (4), you might also think through the actions you intend to take. Be honest and open-minded about it. Test the materials against your own knowledge and experience, and then make up your own mind. But do make up your mind. Use what is convincing and appropriate. Ignore what is unconvincing or unsuitable.

Whatever the outcome, continue to think and continue to strive to develop yourself and those for whom you are responsible. It matters to you, to them and to your organization.

Chapter Two
An introduction to continuous development
Sue Wood, Harry Barrington and Ron Johnson

Continuous development is not a body of theory, nor a collection of techniques: it is an approach to management. Continuous development means:

– learning from real experiences at work
– learning throughout working life, compared with useful but occasional injections of 'training'.

Continuous development is the integration of learning with work. Each member of the team who wrote this book is a missionary – but don't stop reading – since each believes deeply that it is through learning that individuals (and, concomitantly, organizations) grow and become mature. That is, it is the way in which individuals become able to contribute to society, both inside and outside employment, to the fullest extent, by exercising their potential to *its* fullest extent. The terms 'education', 'training' and 'development' are each subsumed by 'learning', the term used almost entirely throughout this book.

The following sections in this chapter are intended to provide the backdrop against which to view subsequent, more specific, chapters.

1 Continuous development – a definition

A general definition of 'continuous development' is difficult to formulate. Individuals can and properly should create their own definitions. The concept is not abstract nor in any way unreal, but each individual will arrive at a personal understanding of the term through his or her experiences which, of course, will be determined by unique, changing circumstances.

John Manager, in charge of a brand in a marketing orientated organization, may at a given moment be concerned about the lack of flexibility within his organization's production units, which is constraining him from relaunching his brand in, say, five colours. He may see continuous development as linked to making the factory more versatile, while at the same time developing the creative instincts in his assistant brand managers to produce advertising ideas which will give the brand a varied image without those five colours. For him, continuous development could mean, for the time being, more instruction in the factories and less instruction in the brand office.

His wife, Jean Manager, managing a library in the Home Counties, might be wrestling with problems of staff cuts and simultaneous increases in clients. Her definition of continuous development might emphasize 'self development' via the introduction of a computerized index facility which both library staff and clients would need to master.

A year later, John and Jean may have moved beyond these problems and opportunities, and have new priorities – which will in turn influence their view of what continuous development means. The only consistent elements in the definitions are likely to be a concern for some sort of improvement, and some sort of learning to that end. People who adopt a continuous development approach properly describe their approach not in theoretical but in 'operational' terms – and they acknowledge that their own understanding of the term 'continuous development' evolves in a unique way.

The case examples which appear later in this book demonstrate the range of individuals' understanding of continuous development in practice. Indeed, several people who helped prepare the case examples have suggested that whilst the 'theory' of continuous development practised by their own organization and maybe a couple of other organizations included in that chapter is 'correct', the others haven't quite got the point yet!

It is not necessary, nor is it possible, to create a rigid set of *laws of continuous development* but it is worth considering some elements of continuous development which can be expected to be apparent in successful examples of its application.

Continuous development (from now on 'CD') *is*:

– the integration of learning with work

Almost without exception, workers at all levels, whether shop-floor workers, supervisors or senior managers, regularly need to learn something new. That 'something new' might be connected with the performance of work tasks, or with the organization of work, or with interrelationships with fellow workers.

Each unsatisfied learning need will have an adverse effect on work performance. All workers want to do their jobs well, for personal satisfaction or in order to gain promotion or merely to keep their jobs, and all learning is the responsibility of the learner.

Most organizations make provision for employees to learn; in particular, provision will be made to enable employees to learn those things which directly affect productivity or the 'bottom line'. Some learning needs are generic but that does not mean to say that the need can be met in some standardized way (see Chapter Six, on how adults learn). Some learning needs can be anticipated, but most cannot. The individual's job itself and the job environment will present the job holder with challenges (the 'something new') which he or she must deal with. Meeting the challenge and learning from it, and using the new knowledge, skill or understanding, is the essence of CD.

– self directed learning

CD *is not* self development (although it may include self development). It *is* self directed learning.

We have seen how both John and Jean Manager may wish to direct learning to serve 'operational' goals. Both may establish strategies to this end without waiting for a superior to tell them what to do. Jim Manager, John's brother, who has just taken up a new position in his firm (and has moved house in the process) may well have an induction programme drawn up for him. But he might try to adjust the programme to fit in with his house moving, and he might equally add to or strengthen items which he feels assume more knowledge than he already has. Jim's daughter Jenny, who hopes to open a restaurant somewhere near their new home, is busy learning about sources of labour and catering training establishments in the area.

The job holder is uniquely placed to understand his or her learning needs. Given a particular learning need and a particular individual and his or her circumstances there will be an optimum means of meeting the need.

It is, however, extremely likely that initially most individuals will require help in thinking in terms of 'learning needs' and then in identifying them. Having identified one's learning needs, individuals are, again initially, extremely likely to need help in planning how to meet those needs.

John Manager talks with senior and middle level factory management (and a factory training officer) about plans for factory workers; and he brings in from an advertising agency a colleague with more experience than he has on brainstorming and synectics techniques. Jean Manager asks the suppliers of the computerized index system how other purchasers have been helped to use the system. Jim Manager asks for a session with his new boss to discuss his own opinions on the draft induction programme. Jenny Manager visits the Jobcentre, the Careers Office and the Catering College.

It may be cost and quality effective for the organization to design or buy a common course for a group of employees; there may be a distance learning package available which precisely matches a need. It is increasingly likely, however, given the rate and degree of change in the workplace, that an individual's learning needs will be unique: thus he or she must learn a little about learning in order to understand learning options and make the best possible choice between them. A learning plan may include: course or college attendance; working through open or distance learning materials; reading, listening or observing. The learner's choice will depend upon what he or she wants to learn and how, and on both self-imposed and externally imposed constraints (for example, job demands, employer attitude, family duties, the availability of appropriate learning materials).

An early aim of the CD process is to enable individuals themselves to identify learning needs and opportunities and to decide how best to meet and exploit them. Thus, although in the beginning personnel professionals or line managers will need to assist other workers to come to terms with the CD concept (having come to terms with it themselves, of course), once the process is established each learner can become the director of his or her own learning.

– a process, not a technique

CD *is not* a new way of tackling old problems, nor the latest North American management import, guaranteed to solve all your management problems. The popularity of such techniques tends to be short-lived, no matter how sensible and well tried and tested they are. Perhaps this is because they *are* techniques, that is, externally imposed and only indirectly part of 'getting the job done', not part and parcel of the job itself. Those who have seen fads and fashions and supposed revolutions in training and development come and go are inclined to be cynical when confronted with the latest cure-all technique.

John, Jean, Jim and Jenny Manager must all work at their self directed learning processes; their level of commitment is more likely to determine the outcome than any specific techniques they may use.

CD is not a technique – and it *is not* for certain sectors only, nor for certain categories of worker only. All workers can adopt the CD attitude. Simply put, 'Let me think about what I'm doing. Can I do it better, quicker? What's changed since yesterday? Can I learn from that? Who can help me?' is an attitude far from being for managers only. Managers are, however, the key group of workers who can introduce the CD philosophy into their organizations. Personnel professionals have a role to play but the support of line managers is absolutely crucial to the effective introduction of the CD process.

– an attitude, a way of tackling work

The individual and the organization must work at CD to make it real. There is no manual. Two organizations or two people in one department in one organization may well apply CD quite differently, quite legitimately. Self-evidently, operational needs differ from organization to organization, from department to department and from individual to individual; and they also differ over time. Once CD is introduced into the system, via the people who operate that system, it cannot be eradicated. Learning will become a habit; thinking positively about problems, that is, viewing them as opportunities for learning, is a great deal more comfortable than worrying about them and hiding them on the top shelf.

> John Manager did not wait for the company's operating plan to tell him that some new learning plans were needed; Jean Manager did not wait for the equipment supplier to suggest the way ahead; Jim Manager made his induction programme one that *he* owned, not one handed down to him; Jenny Manager went out to manage the environment before the environment managed her. In fact, they all *managed* – because they had a CD attitude.

> The 'CD attitude' frees individuals from misguided dependence on some 'authority', be it a teacher, a book, a homily. It allows workers to become increasingly self-reliant – which includes saying 'I don't know the answer. How can I find out?'

– simultaneous improvement in the performance of employees and organizations

The CD process helps individuals to develop, and thus helps the organization to achieve its objectives, through the intimate association of improved learning and improved performance.

Every worker, even a self-employed individual, is part of a team or teams. It is important that each individual understands the contribution he or she is expected to make to the variety of teams he or she belongs to (and to recognize his or her membership of the range of teams he or she belongs to). Learning in groups and from groups of fellow workers is a powerful factor in the process of the effective management of change, whatever the change might be.

CD can be viewed as a system of continuing improvement in the performance of teams. As the team improves so it better exploits the resources at its disposal, be those resources human, monetary or physical (in old-fashioned management terms the three 'm's: 'men, money and materials'). The CD process thus contributes significantly to the optimum return on whatever technology is employed; or in other words, on the capital employed in an enterprise.

2   Continuous development – its evolution and its place

CD, acknowledged or unrecognized, has all but replaced 'systematic training': that is, task analysis carried out by some third party, leading to the setting up of formal training plans. (Systematic, in its everyday sense of 'methodical, according to a plan, not casual or sporadic or unintentional' is a perfectly good description of conscious continuous development. The selection of formal and informal training processes derived from systematic analysis of an individual's learning needs – by the individual or in association with the individual – are desirable outcomes of the CD approach.)

Why has it taken the place of 'systematic training'? For two reasons. The first is the rate and degree of change in the workplace. The second is societal change: people are less willing than they were to accept authority unquestioningly, and more willing to be responsible for themselves. The first point is incontrovertible; the second is controversial, which is perhaps more reason for believing the truth of it. Undoubtedly also the two points are inextricably bound together. A co-author of this book, Dr Ron Johnson, characterizes CD this way: 'The world is changing, I must change with it and, if I can, stay one step ahead of the game'. Another co-author, Harry Barrington, traces the evolution of the training process through several stages:

the 'systematic approach', that is, task analysis leading to formal training plans;

the 'dynamic approach', that is, employee appraisal informed (ideally) by an organizationally driven overview of strategy and objectives, leading to improved, *individual*, performance plans;

the 'CD approach', that is, the adoption of the CD attitude leading to the integration of learning with work.

In the early development of UK training systems, operations and learning tended to be separated. In the early fifties, training was generally restricted to newcomers entering a limited range of jobs: craft, secretarial and junior management jobs were those most frequently understood to carry 'initial' training programmes. The method of creating the programmes was, in the jargon of the times, 'systematic'. Typically, a job description (which described the tasks to be performed) was written, and from it a job specification (which listed the knowledge and skill requirements) was drawn up. Then the job specification was transformed into a training specification, which was a set of plans whereby the newcomer, who was assumed to have *no* knowledge and *no* skill, was put through a number of experiences from which he or she was expected to acquire both. Training was planned to precede work – or at least to happen away from it, very shortly after appointment.

During the fifties, this systematic approach was extended to other jobs: for example, to sales staff, office staff, process staff, and so on. When the Industry Training Boards appeared in the early sixties, they preached 'systematic training' as though it were a natural law. The task of producing the training specifications demanded by the ITBs was usually undertaken by a personnel or training officer or manager, working within a personnel department, although these people were often aided by substantial input from work study observers, who contributed the products of their method study work.

It is important to realize that this approach was – and indeed, still is – essentially a static one. Job descriptions described the job *at the time it was studied*; job specifications outlined *current* knowledge and skill needs; the training specification assumed training was completed at the end of the programme. What is more, the person who was to be trained was not a party to the training plan; he or she would benefit from it only by conforming to it (some plans even included early experiences designed to secure 'motivation' towards the plan).

The sixties were not happy days for most UK companies. Overseas markets shrank, and an increasingly adverse balance of payments led to attempts to curb internal spending. Improved productivity became a major aim; but trade union activity tended to resist workplace changes and force high wage increases. It was also the time during which 'Management by Objectives' flourished, and Drucker's idea of 'managing the future today' became widely accepted. In this climate, personnel and training staff moved naturally into the 'improved performance' field, developing, for example, new appraisal systems which yielded training objectives (and often divorced appraisal from pay), and creating training plans which were aimed at established staff rather than newcomers (the flow of which was beginning to dry up).

The key point here is that learning aims were beginning to be derived from operational analyses, and the workforce as a whole was no longer being viewed as competent on the basis of initial, 'systematic' training activity. Almost as important was the contribution of line managers to identifying training needs; the static job descriptions and job specifications tended to be ignored in the discussion of what should be improved.

The operational need for improved performance dramatically increased in the mid seventies following the surge in the oil price and a period of rampant inflation. Survival became a prime concern, and short term objectives overtook long term objectives as the driving force. Recruitment was cut back further as organizations concluded – despite trade union resistance – that overmanning was one of the major millstones affecting commercial results. Redundancies became a natural feature of the UK employment scene; some training managers were among the first to go. Personnel managers became involved in discussions about new organizational devices to improve performance: briefing groups, joint productivity planning committees, value analysis teams, study groups and (later) quality circles, found their way into the world of work. This was industry *learning how to learn* – not by 'training' but through management action.

The seventies were also times when the idea of worker participation and involvement flourished. Since many of the new structures spread across departmental boundaries, traditional lines of command weakened, and collective innovation was seen as something to be cultivated. Organizational development ('OD') activities included many explicitly aimed at improving the confidence of all levels of the workforce in order to share in the total operation. Management now became as much to do with helping the system to develop itself as with taking decisions and passing them down the line.

In this climate, the word 'training' became steadily less appropriate as a description of how the organization managed its learning function. The word 'development', long used to describe improved performance for managers, tended to replace it.

'Training plans' became increasingly strategic, linked to new work patterns, smaller workforces and changed responsibilities. This change accelerated with the rush of technological innovations which emerged in the late seventies and eighties. The silicon chip produced a revolution in machine methods of all kinds; the computer allowed fast data, fast decisions, and fast communication; optic fibres allowed greatly increased communicability. Technologists worked with line managers to agree new equipment proposals, and to incorporate in commissioning plans proposals which involved learning on the part of those who were not redundant. When the equipment arrived, it was sometimes 'adapted' at the workplace in order to perform unique functions; hence more learning requirements, which the manufacturers could only rarely cover, and which were usually handled at the workplace without any mention in corporate training plans.

Faced with the acceleration of technological change, personnel departments tended to abandon the creation of detailed plans, concentrating instead on (a) manpower strategies; (b) negotiations with unions – increasingly amicable and increasingly dealing with development, as the impact of the technological revolution became evident; (c) providing learning resources; and (d) stimulating the idea of self development, especially for managers. 'Training Managers' became 'Employee Development Managers' (with *all* staff, including managers, being included in the term 'employee'); personnel management became for some people 'human resource development': for some exceptional people it always had been. Developing people and work simultaneously had become a central feature of the personnel role, but one which left the decisions and the planning of learning where it mattered – at the workplace, with contributions from all levels on a self help basis. Continuous development had arrived.

3   Continuous development – IPM's involvement

It was in the climate described above that the IPM's National Committee for Training and Development (NCTD) discussed a variety of documents which purported to offer neat solutions to the problem of the UK's poor economic performance. These documents had certain features in common, all issuing from bodies at national level, and all suggesting a central prescription: if the world of work would conform to some 'best model', recovery would be achievable. Time after time, the NCTD said 'it just isn't like that'; members saw the essence of what was happening as organic development, which properly allowed millions of unique improvements to be devised *and managed* at the workplace without having to conform to someone else's idea of what would be good for the average operation.

This was the genesis of the IPM's ABCD (A Boost for Continuous Development) Campaign of which this book is one element. CD philosophy as it has emerged is essentially a commentary on how business and management has naturally evolved in the past half century, and particularly over the last dozen years: from stability to dynamism, from descriptions to objectives, from systemization to creativity, from management command to participative decision, from teaching to learning. To summarize, from *training alongside* work to *learning within* it.

'Employee development' is the subject of one third of the IPM's currrent qualifying examinations. Although the system of examinations may change and although it may be that examinations themselves will be replaced or supplemented by improved measures of competence, the need for personnel professionals to understand continuous development will remain. First, personnel professionals themselves need to continue to learn; second, personnel professionals need to advise line managers on human resource management – the full exploitation of the human resources of an enterprise – the heart of which is continuous development.

CD has already begun to make its appearance in IPM examination papers and has given many students a problem. Most examinations are designed to test knowledge and understanding. Most of the questions in IPM examination papers can fairly confidently be attempted by anyone who has carefully read selected texts or who has listened to lecturers or practising personnel managers, and, at least, memorized the information (ideally, understood it as well). The CD questions are different in as much as they require the student to reflect on his or her own experience and draw conclusions from it. There are no experts, no gurus, no received wisdom, just 'What would you do/did you do, and why? With what results? What did you learn?' Few of us have the confidence, or indeed any experience, in putting forward our own views as *the* answer in an examination. But this is exactly what is required here.

Experienced managers know that effective management is the art of 'managing contingency with expediency', or, much better stated, thinking for oneself and acting quickly on one's decision. Text books and the host of management taxonomies certainly help intending managers to learn the basic language of management (including personnel management). If management competence were expressed on a scale from 1 to 5, where 1 is lowest, those who relied simply upon this learning of the language of management would probably reach level 1.

The authors hope that this book will be helpful to the IPM's Student Members in coming to terms with the concept of CD: the following sub-section has been written with them in mind. Many managers express the view that they learn most by reflecting on some topic and then discussing it with colleagues. Students may choose to read the following and then arrange to meet with fellow students to discuss their understanding of it.

The concept of continuous development: students' brief

The concept of continuous development has not been consciously built up from a theoretical base but rather from practical experience and the testing of theories and models. It has been developed as a practical approach to enable people at work to maintain their effectiveness in the midst of an ever-changing situation. Although the rationale for CD has emerged from the day to day experiences of practitioners, it is consistent with the findings of research into organizational behaviour and the way people learn and adapt to change. (See 'Further Reading'.)

Those Training Managers who have adopted the CD approach have done so because they perceive that a dynamic, proactive attitude and approach is needed to enable individuals and organizations to spot and use the opportunities inherent in change. Moreover, the approach works. The key to the concept is the need to go on learning, and to embrace learning as a way of life; something that can happen each day, and probably should. In everyday life, learning is not something that happens only when you attend classes: it happens when you listen to the radio or watch TV, read the newspapers or listen to other people talking, cope with a difficult situation or work out how to use a new gadget. The idea which the IPM's CD approach emphasizes is that managers should *expect* learning to occur all the time: people should be looking out for opportunities to learn, and for opportunities to help their colleagues and subordinates to learn. Opportunities for learning at the workplace occur all the time. But this is not enough. Managers must also be on the look-out for occasions when *they* need to seek out new knowledge, understanding and skills if they are to succeed in improving performance.

CD is concerned with improvements which are consciously promoted or managed, rather than changes which take place in a random or sporadically reactive fashion. The CD approach emphasizes the interrelationships between the technical and the personnel aspects of day to day operations, and also the need to develop in parallel the technology and the competence of people. Hence, CD can be described as an approach to management which strives constantly for improvements relating both to organizational achievements and to people's competence.

(Alternatively, CD might be described as a socio-technical system.) In order to translate such ideas into reality within an organization, the lead must be given from the top. And those who take the trouble to learn and to promote learning need encouragement and support from their superiors.

The CD approach is based on two sets of ideas: first, 'what managers need to learn and how this can be accomplished'; and secondly, 'how organizations can promote these concepts and the practical implementation of ongoing learning and development'. Students may find it helpful to look at research and other work in these two key areas. (See 'Further Reading'.)

'What managers need to learn and how this can be accomplished'

Neglect of the management development needs of middle managers was highlighted in Alistair Mant's *The experienced manager* (1). Drawing on a substantial research base, in 1980 the Manpower Services Commission concluded that 'managing and learning are not opposed' (2). Reg Revans highlighted the ways in which managers can learn from each other, from their experiences and through the challenges they face in the workplace (3). The importance of learning on and from the job through coaching was emphasized by Edwin Singer (4).

Although the literature on learning in general is extensive, there has been less research into learning by managers *per se*. A number of useful concepts have been put forward by Kolb, and by Honey and Mumford (5). There has also been much interest recently in the manager's ability to take responsibility for his or her own learning (6). Taken together, these writings emphasize the fact that successful managers learn throughout their working lives, and that much of this learning can take place at the workplace and through the medium of work. The various authors also emphasize the fact that as managers become more conscious of the learning process and ways in which they can accelerate and capitalize on their learning, their motivation to work and to learn, and their effectiveness as managers, increases.

'How organizations can promote these concepts and the practical implementation of ongoing learning and development'

The complex web of information flows and interactions which characterizes modern organizations, and the research on how these work, have been summarized by Charles Handy (7). What is clear is that the behaviour of managers at work is profoundly influenced by the organizational climate, by what is perceived as being valued by the organization, and by what actions are rewarded by the organization.

These two strands of research underpin continuous development. It may be useful at this stage to read through the CD Code, 'Continuous Development: People and Work', which is reproduced in full as Chapter Three of this book.

The Code summarizes the essential features of CD as being the need for managers to promote:

- workplace learning and self development
- the integration of learning with work and improved performance.

'Workplace learning and self development'

Hitherto, learning has been achieved mainly through pre-planned training designed to equip each individual with a set of knowledge and skills that would enable him or her to undertake the tasks required by the organization.

Individuals can no longer rely on 'an expert' marshalling facts and information for them and passing it on in appropriate packages. Individuals are increasingly thrown upon their own resources. Organizations require managers and workers who can adapt to and anticipate change, and this means that more attention must be paid to learning processes. Although many of the learning steps are individually small, taken over a period they can amount to a considerable degree of development. As the focus shifts away from training and towards learning, the initiative for learning also moves away from the trainers and towards the *learners*.

Thus managers are encouraged to take increasing responsibility for their own learning, and, in turn, to encourage their subordinates to accept more responsibility for their own development. For many managers this is a major shift, and one which will not take place quickly, nor without leadership, encouragement and support. Before managers and other employees can take appropriate initiatives related to their development, it is vital that they understand how their roles within the organization are developing; how their work fits into the overall picture; and how improvement in their own effectiveness brings them rewards in the broadest sense. Once there is motivation to learn specific things there may well be a need for training experts to assist managers in deciding the best methods for learning and the appropriate mix of on-the-job and off-the-job activities to achieve the desired results.

'The integration of learning with work and improved performance'

There are many activities where learning takes place in a work context: for example, information is imparted or exchanged at briefing sessions, business meetings and appraisal interviews. Many managers do not see this as learning.

There is a need to integrate learning and work: for many managers, learning is something that takes place elsewhere, away from and only tangentially related to the workplace. Hence when crises arise or time is short, learning activities are among the first to be sacrificed. Ironically, crises provide rich opportunities for learning and, for many people, are often the most fruitful learning experiences and generally the most memorable. Taking time out after such events to review what took place and why, and how such matters can be dealt with more effectively in the future, would enable managers to benefit to a much greater degree from these real life experiences. Further, such reflections will help people, next time, to experience the learning at the same time as solving the problem, not merely learning by looking back.

At the simplest level, they may have learned how to avoid the particular problem in the future, not just how to cope with it.

To sum up, consider the organization as:

- a group of people
- interrelated within an organization structure
- together performing tasks
- with a set of tools and technologies.

It is possible to analyse an organization by considering each of these four factors, the way in which they are related, and how the environment affects each of them.

An analysis of this sort will quickly reveal that to be effective, the people concerned must be competent at their own tasks, not only on an individual basis, but also in terms of the inter-group interactions involved. This highlights the need for learning to be undertaken not only at the individual level, but at the level of the working team, and also at the interfaces or boundaries (which could be multi-faceted) where the teams interact. Thus CD is not just about helping individuals to learn but also about enabling teams of individuals to secure organizational growth.

4 Continuous development – introducing it into the organization

Finding examples of 'CD in practice' for this book was difficult at first. Few organizations use the term although very many recognize the descriptions of what CD *is* (see above), as being what they actually practise. CD was not invented by the IPM, it existed already; it is not a theory, but a belief founded on experience and reflection. The IPM hopes to codify the principles of CD and to spread the good news of its discovery.

CD – the integration of learning with work – has emerged spontaneously, often in response to adversity. Individuals, especially managers, in organizations faced with dangerous external competition, skilled labour shortages, increased demand for services, radical technological change, changes in working practices, or a combination of all of these factors, have

been and are being obliged to introduce an environment which
enables and encourages employees to learn and to learn fast. It
is necessary, however, for such individuals to recognize adversity as an opportunity. It is, of course, quite possible that those
who are responsible for the organization of a work unit will try
to solve the new problem in the old way. It is highly likely, however, that the CD approach will bring rewards to the organization simply in the form of the fuller exploitation of resources (in
particular, human resources). The CD approach relies upon
the flexibility of work systems and presents a number of
challenges. For example:

> Team working must actively be fostered; this is likely to
> concertina the chain of command. The more that teams of
> people are made fully responsible for some work operation,
> the less necessary it will be to maintain a hierarchy of super-
> visors. The efficient communication of sound personnel
> policies will become even more important.
>
> Each individual's learning should be viewed as contribut-
> ing to the overall effectiveness of the team. Individuals
> within work teams must determine learning priorities and
> negotiate their fulfilment.
>
> Individuals tend not to be rewarded for their effort, but
> rather for the effectiveness of their performance. Rational
> and credible performance appraisal systems which both
> reward and motivate continuous developers must be insti-
> tuted and maintained.
>
> If individuals are to contribute fully, and grow in their
> jobs, rigid job descriptions are likely to be inappropriate. Job
> descriptions should be dated (and updated when appro-
> priate), and written in terms of key results.

CD is probably most easily introduced as a concomitant of
some obvious and concrete change; for example, a geographical
move, expansion into a new product range or the closure of a
site. In this way, all workers will recognize the need for, and be
prepared for, change. Such changes are not hard to find, or even
to manufacture.

All changes offer learning opportunities but not all are good
news to all employees. An employee faced with redundancy will,

however, only be helped by an introduction to the CD attitude: if it does not help him or her to retrain for a job with the present organization it may well assist him or her to find alternative employment or to use his or her special talents outside employment.

Clearly, personnel departments have a role to play in introducing CD within organizations but it is the line manager and particularly senior line managers who will determine by their own attitudes and behaviour whether CD will be introduced successfully. For example, employees who are encouraged to take 'a broad view' and to take risks in reaching for distant goals will not co-operate if it is simultaneously made evident that the rewards for success are inadequate or that the punishment for failure is unacceptable.

CD must not be laid down as a challenge. It will suit some employees to reach for the sky, and such people are very valuable, certainly as catalysts. The majority of employees are more conservative and must not feel threatened by too competitive an environment. Hence the importance of the concept of team working: each member of a team (formally or informally constituted) contributes uniquely and thus each member has value to the overall effectiveness of the team. Individual members of a team who do not pull their weight are more likely to improve as a result of peer group pressure than through externally imposed sanctions.

As CD means different things to different people, so there is no one best way of introducing it into the organization. Nonetheless, as a general formula, it is likely that organizations will proceed through the following steps:

- a recognition of the opportunity to introduce CD

- a decision to seize the opportunity

- a commitment to the concept, from the top of the organization

- communication of the ideas to all employees in traditional and new ways (for example through company newspapers, or by including in job advertisements mention of the organization's commitment to learning)

- creation of opportunities for employees to learn about learning

- creation of formal support systems (for example, an appropriate appraisal system, clear policies on off-the-job training or the availability of training materials)

- formation of formal and informal work groups dedicated to mutual support in solving problems or improving performance

- regular review and attention to maintenance/repair/renewal of the systems which emerge.

The next chapter gives more specific advice to those who want to introduce CD into their organization, division, or department.

To some extent, the principles of CD are already in evidence (somewhere) in most organizations. The short questionnaire which follows is intended to help you to decide where your organization lies along a notional spectrum, where:

0 = no CD in evidence, and 15 = full commitment to CD

and so to decide how much work there is to do, and what use can be made of the contents of this book. (First complete the questionnaire and then read on, at the top of page 28.)

CD 'rating' questionnaire

A. Philosophy and Policy

1 ● Does your organization already have a statement or statements of belief/purpose relating to the management of people and explicitly including a corporate commitment to what could be termed 'continuous development'?

2 ● Do managers in your organization generally know 'who carries responsibility for what' in the identification of learning aims and the promotion of learning activity?

B. Strategy and Forward Plans

3 ● Are the organization's strategic plans available to all managers?

4 ● Do they include items explicitly addressing such things as improved performance, new methods and equipment, and organizational change?

5 ● Must new capital proposals contain an outline of resulting training needs?

C. Identification of Learning Opportunities and Needs

6 ● Do you at this moment know what are your own and your department's priority learning needs?

7 ● Does your organization promote special group arrangements such as Quality Circles, Joint Productivity Planning Committees, Value Analysis Teams, Study Groups, etc.

D. Learner Involvement

8 ● Do *informal* appraisal discussions take place regularly to establish new 'self development' aims?

9 ● Do standing committees regularly include on their agendas an item involving review of their purpose and effectiveness?

10 ● Do departments/units organize 'process review' sessions in which staff review their own achievements and problems?

E. Learning Resources

11 ● Do training budgets exist?

12 ● Do managers generally know who has authority to approve learning plans and expenditure?

13 ● Do employees at all levels have facilities for study during standard working hours?

F. The Overall Culture

14 ● Do all members, management and non-management, appear to understand and share ownership of operational goals?

15 ● Do people appear to learn while they work, and to enjoy both?

	YES	NO
1.		
2.		
3.		
4.		
5.		
6.		
7.		
8.		
9.		
10.		
11.		
12.		
13.		
14.		
15.		

Score ONE mark for each question to which you can honestly answer YES.

The best way is probably to create your own personal strategy. This demands:

- coming to terms with the contents page

- 'skimming' the chapters to appreciate what each covers and how each is presented

- deciding which parts are your 'first interest'

- creating your own list of *learning objectives* (eg what you want to be able to explain later, what you want to be able to do later, what you want to judge as valuable or otherwise)

- devising an 'order of play' which combines objectives and interest, and establishes clearly in your mind how you will assess your learning progress.

Creating such a learning strategy is not easy: most of us have left this sort of thing to the teachers and trainers in the past – and it is arguable that many teachers and trainers have failed to do it, or at least to explain it adequately. So – here are three possible strategies, each linked with a particular score on the questionnaire you have just completed.

STRATEGY A – for those who scored 12 AND OVER

If you have scored over 12, you can confidently conclude that you work in an organization that already has substantial commitment to CD (whether or not the term is used). Whilst you may search Chapter Three for specifics to develop, your best approach may be to:

(a) select those cases in Chapter Four which you feel reflect similar types of organization or operation to your own, and 'compare notes'

(b) work through the relevant Prompt List(s) in Chapter Five to sharpen your appreciation of your own CD culture.

Chapter Six, on Learning Skills, should give you some pointers for future self development activity in promoting your understanding of learning.

STRATEGY B – for those who scored BETWEEN 6 and 11

If you have scored between 6 and 11, you clearly have *some* CD activity around you, but also a lot of new options to explore. Your best approach may be to:

(a) explore the relevant Prompt List(s) in Chapter Five first – not to memorize the answers given, but merely to establish for yourself the extent to which you have clear ideas about what CD is all about

(b) go through Chapter Three, highlighting the elements that are *not* currently part of your organization's culture, and choosing those which you would like to see developed

(c) read all the cases in Chapter Four, searching for examples of what you would like to see in action

(d) tackle the Prompt List(s) in Chapter Five again, building your new goals into the answers

(e) make a conscious attempt to build *into your work role* responsibility for progressing the goals you have established

(f) read Chapter Six with a clear intent to use its material to help your own self development towards achieving (e).

STRATEGY C – for those who scored LESS THAN 6

If you have scored less than 6, read the book as it is presented (but don't waste too much time on any individual Chapter Four case example which you find unrelated to or remote from your organization). Then start again, using the strategy suggested for those who scored between 6 and 12.

Chapter Three
'Continuous Development: People and Work' – a statement
Harry Barrington and Sue Wood

Introduction

The IPM's ABCD (A Boost for Continuous Development) campaign was launched in 1984. The campaign's ambitious aim is to change individuals' and organizations' attitudes to learning. As a first step, a summary of the principles of continuous development was produced for IPM members in the form of an IPM Statement. It became clear very quickly that IPM members recognized the potential of the CD approach. It was also clear that respondents fell into two distinct groups. One group of people wanted to see a theoretical justification of CD; a second group wanted to be able to obtain practical material which would enable them to introduce CD within their organizations. One reaction would have been to decide that such respondents had not grasped the meaning nor implications of the CD approach. The IPM's team did not react in this way: first because they themselves are not above learning and if the reactions received showed a gap in understanding there was clearly a fault in the communication itself; second because they believed that they could offer more help than generalized advice. Two results are this book and, specifically, this chapter. The Statement reproduced here is the third edition of that first attempt to begin a dialogue on the subject of CD.

'Continuous development: People and Work'

1   Introduction and aims

Continuous development is not a body of theory, nor a collection of techniques: it is an approach to the management of learning. Continuous development means:

learning from real experiences at work
learning throughout working life, not confined to useful but occasional injections of 'training'.

For the individual, CD means lifelong learning with a strong element of self-direction and self-management. For the organization, CD means the management of learning on a continuing basis through the promotion of learning as an integtral part of work itself.

An organization's success depends upon its people. If the organization is to become more successful, employee learning must be stimulated and managed – not specifically and separately, but constantly – in relation to all work activities. The essential basis for this management is not a set of prescribed techniques but an attitude of mind; it is this attitude which justifies the CD label and generates the desired growth.

This Statement, 'Continuous Development: People and Work', is designed to help all managers, especially personnel professionals, to broaden their views about learning and training, to help them to anchor their learning activity firmly in the organization's day to day activities, and – most important of all – to promote the development of the CD attitude. The IPM considers that such a Statement is necessary because, in the UK, training has too rarely been thought of as a continuous process. Rather, it has been treated as a series of short term expedients; and usually in reaction to change, not in anticipation of it.

These issues are further explored in the Code under seven key headings, as follows:

The essential conditions for a CD culture; Policy; Responsibilities and roles; The identification of learning opportunities and needs; The integration of learning with work; The provision of learning resources; Benefits and results.

2   The essential conditions for a CD culture

If learning activity is to be fully beneficial to both the organization and its employees, the following conditions must be met:

- the organization must have some form of strategic operational plan – and the implications of this plan should be spelt out in terms of the knowledge, skills and concerns of all employees

- managers must be ready, willing and able to define, give priority to, and meet learning needs as they appear. Not all such needs can be anticipated. In the early stages of developing the CD culture, encouragement must be given to employees to suggest learning needs from the problems and challenges, and the successes and failures, encountered in their day to day activities

- learning and work must be integrated.This means *both* (a) dovetailing plans for learning with other operational plans, *and* (b) devising and maintaining systems and processes which stimulate learning activity. But it also means, wherever possible, arranging work activities which themselves incorporate a learning element

- the impetus for CD must come from the Chief Executive and other members of the top management team. They must regularly and formally review the way in which the competence of both management and the workforce are being developed. In the early stages, one senior executive should be charged with overall responsibility for overseeing the practical aspects of introducing CD

- investment in CD must be regarded by the top management team as being as important as investment in research, new product development or capital equipment. This investment – in terms of both time and money – is not a luxury which can only be afforded in the 'good times'. Indeed, the more severe the problems an organization faces the greater the need for learning on the part of its employees and the more pressing the need for investment in learning.

Successful CD demands:

- rapid and effective communication of priority operational needs

- the availability of appropriate learning opportunities, facilities and resources as a normal part of working life

- processes which naturally integrate learning with work

- recognition by each employee that he or she shares ownership of any collective learning plans to meet the priority operational needs

- recognition by each employee that he or she has a responsibility to communicate and otherwise share new information, again with the purpose of meeting priority operational needs

- recognition by each employee that he or she is able to and allowed to create a personal development plan

- a clear understanding, by everyone in the organization, of their responsibilities for learning.

3 Policy

Most organizations find statements of policy useful. Any statement of general policy relating to the management of people should indicate:

- a firm corporate commitment to continuous development

- that self development is a responsibility of every individual within the organization

- the need for employees, clients and customers to understand as much as possible about how individuals and groups of people learn, and why it is important

- the organization's commitment to acknowledge improved performance, to use enhanced skills operationally, and to provide appropriate rewards

- 'who carries responsibility for what' in the identification of learning aims and the promotion of learning activity

- ways in which operational aims and objectives are communicated to all employees

- agreed procedures and methods for performance appraisal and assessment

- avenues, procedures and processes for career development and progression

- facilities provided for learning during work time, including paid or unpaid leave for this purpose

- the organization's policy on employee involvement, especially that relating to involvement in reviewing education and training facilities and resources

If the statement of general policy is not to be a sterile document of mere good intent:

- top management must be committed to it and should periodically request feedback on its implementation

- senior executives and middle and junior level managers must be given the opportunity to suggest amendments in line with what they regard as 'current operational reality'

- The document must regularly be discussed with representatives of the workforce

- the organization must satisfy itself that it is making best use of the research and development findings in the human resource development fields, (and perhaps get involved with such research activity).

4   Responsibilities and roles

All members in the organization should be able to view the operational life of the organization as a continuous learning process: and one in which they all carry responsibilities.

Senior executives have the responsibility to ensure that policy statements and practices promote CD and that forward plans incorporate future management needs, particularly to improve performance – taking into account the impact of key changes in legal requirements, technology, work patterns and (not least) ideas. They must encourage managers to plan learning activities to facilitate the process of change.

Managers as part of their responsibilities for getting the best out of their staff, must give regular attention to subordinates' continuous development: discussing needs, creating plans, coaching, mentoring, counselling, introducing changes which make learning easier and/or more effective. Managers must engender their own 'learning about learning'.

Personnel professionals have very many responsibilities in the CD field. They should provide an information service on resources, and continuously monitor the extent and quality of learning activity in the organization. If they feel that the learning activity is inadequate to support the operational needs of the business, they should take the initiative in generating strategic and/or tactical discussions, recommending appropriate action as necessary. They should ensure that review discussions happen at least once a year within the senior executive group and within any consultative groups. Internal personnel department review discussions should take place frequently: personnel professionals must constantly seek to improve their own performance and the service they provide to their organizations.

All learners (including the three groups above) must appreciate that they are responsible for clarifying their own learning goals within the framework established by forward plans, standard procedures and discussions with management. They should raise their problems with management; review their own performance impartially; suggest what they themselves should learn, and how; seek new information without waiting for it to be delivered; alert others whenever important new information is received; ask for explanations whenever a communication is not understood; aim, generally, to use new learning whenever possible. The ultimate aim is for everyone to contribute to the identification of learning opportunities and for learners to manage most of their learning for themselves.

The chief responsibility for *all* learners is to seek constant improvements in performance: no matter the base of 'learning sophistication' from which learners set out, improvement is always possible.

5 The identification of learning opportunities and needs

It is worth repeating that everyone needs to contribute to the indentification of learning opportunities using the information available to them. Some sources of information can be stronger than others, for example:

Operational plans: every proposal for a new operational element, that is, a new product, a new item of plant, a new procedure, a new organization structure, a new department, a new member of staff, a new accounting convention – a new anything, should be accompanied by an estimate of:

which employees need to learn something
what needs to be learned
how the learning is to happen

If these things cannot be defined with confidence, the proposal should include a plan which allows this to be completed later. Some needs are indirectly related: for example, new technical systems may demand not merely instruction in the system itself, but also new levels and types of maintenance. Removing existing resources (machines, materials and perhaps people) may also demand a learning plan.

Job descriptions and specifications: documents outlining management responsibilities should normally include references to:

the roles as appraiser, counsellor, tutor
the responsibility to develop an understanding of
learning processes
the manager's responsibility to include learning
elements in operational plans.

All job descriptions and specifications (regardless of level) should also emphasise the job holder's responsibility for self development on a continuing basis.

Appraisal: appraisal should normally include joint appraiser/ appraisee discussions on the extent to which self development is taking place, and again on the implementation of management-inspired learning plans. Ideally, informal appraisal discussions will happen all the time; a standard question would be 'how long is it since we/you/I learned something new at work?'

Special reviews and audits: parts of the learning system should be specially reviewed from time to time. Inter-departmental working parties, joint consultative committees, trainee groups, and, not least, particular individuals, can be charged with collecting data, analysing it, and reporting to senior executives or to personnel management. These reviews are particularly useful in those parts of the learning system where knowledge or awareness needs to be renewed or revived from time to time: 'health and safety' is a good example.

Prompt lists: it is helpful to create lists of questions in a style and in a sequence which will prompt job-holders to think about aspects of the performance of the job which can be improved through new learning or increased awareness. The list should include questions to which no demonstrably 'correct' answer is known but which prompt educated opinion; and also, questions to which the answer will change over time. These lists can be used as the basis of learning needs identification, and/or for one to one and team review discussions which lead to explicit definition of training needs.

6 The integration of learning with work

Learning must be integrated with work: unfocused learning is akin to recreation. When organizing work, 'learning time' should be built in – and not just in the early stages of any development. Formal learning events should always be planned as part of operational work plans, their timing being fixed to minimize impact on other work requirements but their priority being given *equal* weight. A number of organizational devices should be promoted to ensure that employees are naturally involved in the learning process; to that end:

- joint appraiser/appraisee discussions should aim at joint definition of objectives and the means to achieve them

- quality circles, briefing groups, and any other special organizational groupings, should explicitly contain 'improved performance' and 'management of change' aims, and should devote time to discussing the learning aspects of any proposals for future activity

- when new plant or equipment is planned and introduced, suppliers should be encouraged to provide more than just written manuals: active dialogue between suppliers and those who are to operate and maintain the new equipment (including contract staff where appropriate) is needed

- project or work teams should encourage a 'multi-skills' approach to their future operations, playing down divisions between jobs and making the most of the flexibility that goes with increased versatility

- where joint consultative arrangements exist, policies relating to training should regularly be discussed with employee representatives at all levels

- reference should be made to training policies, and to any current learning priorities, in progress reports, house magazines and any other communication channels. Through such channels, every opportunity should be taken to reinforce self development goals.

7 The provision of learning resources

Self development, team learning, and continuous operational development, all require resource material and facilities. The organization should have clear policies and practices on:

- training/learning budgets
- authorities to approve training/learning plans and expenditure
- facilities and support for study during and outside standard working hours, including paid and unpaid leave
- open and distance learning
- financial assistance with courses, travel, books, tapes, and other facilities
- awards and/or scholarships
- access to internal and external advisers, counsellors and facilitators
- coaching and tutorial resources
- management's responsibility to create an environment in which continuous development can prosper and succeed.

All employees should be made aware of these policies and the range of facilities and opportunities for learning which are available. Increasingly, individuals are coming to expect their employers to have policies which enable them to develop their competence, and will choose employing organizations which take learning seriously. Some learning will lead to national vocational qualifications, or part qualifications. Some learning will be required by an individual's professional body (to which the individual will have a natural loyalty). This learning is subsumed by the concept of continuous development and is, indeed, a spur to learning.

8   Benefits and results

Strategic plans, or research and development expenditure, are not expected directly to yield precisely quantifiable benefits. They are a means to an end. So too, expenditure on education, training and development should be regarded as a necessary and calculated investment, yielding consequent 'pay-offs' in terms of enhanced business performance. The following benefits can be expected:

- strategic plans are more likely to be achieved

- ideas will be generated and in a form which relates to operational needs

- everyone in the organization will recognize the need for learning effort on their part if the organization is to succeed in its endeavours and thereby their jobs be made more secure

- by enabling employees to make the most of their talents, the organization will be in a position to deploy individuals most effectively; to fill skills gaps from internal resources; to create and retain a motivated workforce

- and, in general, the organization can expect fewer mistakes, fewer accidents, less waste, higher productivity, higher morale, lower staff turnover, better employee relations, better customer service, and hence, greater returns to the organization.

The major benefits are, first, improved operational performance, and second, the simultaneous development of people and work.

The CD culture has many and varied characteristics, and each individual organization which promotes CD will develop its own unique version. There are, nevertheless, certain key characteristics which are likely to emerge:

- all understand and share ownership of operational goals

- immediate objectives exist and are understood by all

- new developments are promoted; change is constructive, welcomed and enjoyed, not forced and resisted

- managers are frequently to be heard discussing learning with their subordinates and colleagues

- time is found by all the team to work on individual members' problems

- reference documents (manuals, specification sheets, dictionaries and the like) are available to all without difficulty, and are used

- colleagues use each other as a resource

- members of teams do not just swap information; they tackle problems and create opportunities

- team members share responsibility for success or failure; they are not dependent upon one or more leaders

- individuals learn while they work, and enjoy both.

Chapter Four
Case Examples

Keith Lathrope, Harry Barrington, Ron Johnson
and Sue Wood

Introduction

The organizations selected for investigation are a very mixed
collection. The criteria for their selection, which all the following twelve examples met, were simply:

- that the organization was operating a system which the
  researchers considered to be a continuous development
  system
- that there were elements of the organization's practice
  from which a general audience could learn
- that there was a personnel or other manager within the
  organization willing to discuss the organization's foray
  into CD territory openly and frankly.

The examples demonstrate the range of interpretation and
the scale of efficacy of the CD approach. Don't look for a
prescription or a template. Do look for elements within each
example which have a meaning for you in your present
circumstances. The chart which follows is a summary of the
case examples, broken down as follows:

- the organization's principal activities
- size and scale of operation
- financial data
- organization structure
- current human resource development practice
- future challenges.

Read and reflect on each case example separately. Decide for
yourself the order in which you will read them. Note those

41

Reference Chart

	CASE EXAMPLE NO 1	CASE EXAMPLE NO 2	CASE EXAMPLE NO 3	CASE EXAMPLE NO 4
ORGANIZATION	SOAP & DETERGENT INDUSTRY ASSOC. (SDIA)	CIVIL SERVICE/ CABINET OFFICE	WEST BROMWICH BUILDING SOCIETY	NABISCO GROUP LTD
PRINCIPAL ACTIVITIES	Trade Association.	Structured approach to training and development of staff throughout Civil Service.	Normal building society activities – mortgages and investments. Services to users are extending.	Manufacture, marketing and distribution of food products.
SIZE AND SCALE No. of Employees Locations	Over 60 member companies. SDIA Office at Hayes Middlesex.	Over 22,000 managers. A very large number of locations.	25th largest UK building society. 500 employees Head Office and 80 branches.	12,000 employees. 20 factory and office locations.
FINANCE Turnover Profit	Not applicable – non profit-making.	Not applicable.	Not applicable. Assets approx. £500 million.	£500 million + (current profit not known)
ORGANIZATION STRUCTURE	F/t Director General and Council of 15. Various committees, including Education & Training. P/t Training Adviser.	Cabinet Office has its own Training Division. All Civil Service Depts have their own Personnel & Training Divisions.	Complex. Branch Managers are linked to Head Office via HO Development Mgrs. HO Personnel and Training.	US parent company. 3 main divisions – Snacks/ Biscuits/Breakfast Cereals. Group and Division Personnel Units.
CURRENT HUMAN RESOURCES DEVELOPMENT PRACTICES	Established as Non-Statutory Training Organization. Promotion of CD practices.	Various – widespread training activities in many Civil Service departments	Structured initial training for all. Annual training plan and budget. Branch Managers arrange local activities. Weekly 'Training Period' in branches.	Varies throughout the 20 locations.
FUTURE CHALLENGES TO THE ORGANIZATION	Continuing need to keep abreast of national VET developments.	Senior Management Development Programme (SMDP). Annual Update Enquiry.	New services to be provided for users. Review/reform of internal communications. Computerized methods.	Aggressive new product development programme. 'Performance Management.

ORGANIZATION	CASE EXAMPLE NO 5 IDOM	CASE EXAMPLE NO 6 OXFORDSHIRE DISTRICT HEALTH AUTHORITY	CASE EXAMPLE NO 7 TOSHIBA (UK) LTD	CASE EXAMPLE NO 8 BABCOCK ENERGY LTD
PRINCIPAL ACTIVITIES	Consultancy.	Care of the sick.	Manufacture of television sets, video products and microwave ovens.	Manufacture of steam generating plant for power stations.
SIZE AND SCALE No. of Employees Locations	306 employees. Spain.	10,000 employees. 8 units.	1,000 employees. 1 main unit.	8,448 employees. 6 sites.
FINANCE Turnover Profit	1,400m Pesetas. 140m Pesetas.	Not applicable.	£100m turnover.	£282,482,000 in 1985 £5,017,000
ORGANIZATION STRUCTURE	Matrix/co-operative.	Authority, Line Managers.	Board, Line Managers.	Board, Line Managers.
CURRENT HUMAN RESOURCES DEVELOPMENT PRACTICES	Association of professionals which aims to develop people and their competence.	Emphasis on formal training for professional staff – shifting to managers training staff on the job.	Egalitarian: workers learn to carry out work procedures. Emphasis on worker's contribution to high standards.	Usual procedures – job evaluation, job descriptions, appraisals, etc.
FUTURE CHALLENGES TO THE ORGANIZATION	To adapt to changing needs, especially for consultancy in corporate strategy.	To develop the service with limited resources, especially in training.	To maintain the system. Continuing to meet employees' aspirations while still increasing business.	To penetrate new markets other than power stations.

ORGANIZATION	CASE EXAMPLE NO 9 **BANK OF ENGLAND**	CASE EXAMPLE NO 10 **NOBLE LOWNDES & PARTNERS**	CASE EXAMPLE NO 11 **AUSTIN ROVER**	CASE EXAMPLE NO 12 **GROW SOUTH!**
PRINCIPAL ACTIVITIES	Central banking. Market supervision. Policy advice to Government.	Employee benefits and actuarial counselling. Pensions administration. Personal finance.	Motor vehicle manufacture. Component manufacture.	A Local Collaborative Project (LCP). Aim to stimulate more relevant adult training and development.
SIZE AND SCALE No. of Employees Locations	5,000 employees. London and several major UK cities.	1,500 employees worldwide. London, regions and overseas.	12 main factories. 39,000 employees in company. (9,000 at Cowley) 500,000 vehicles produced per year by the company.	Four employees. Office located at South Bank Technopark.
FINANCE Turnover Profit	£88m in 1985/86.	£44m. £8.5m in 1985/86.	Sales: £2,200m per year.	Collaborative partners and Government Depts meet costs.
ORGANIZATION STRUCTURE	Court. Specialist and support functions. Corporate training dept.	Head Office and autonomous regions. Small central training department and personnel.	Subsidiary of Rover Group. Functional operational structure. Small on-site training department.	Steering Group guides unit's work.
CURRENT HUMAN RESOURCES DEVELOPMENT PRACTICES	Structured work based training for all entrants. Professional education. Internal courses. Line responsibility for training.	Strong encouragement of professional education. Line responsibility for training. Link between competence and reward.	Full induction for all. Commitment to work-based learning and int/ext mix of provision. Senior management closely involved in all aspects.	Personnel work as consultants, external interventionists and local team-builders.
FUTURE CHALLENGES TO THE ORGANIZATION	Rapidly changing markets. Supervision and self-regulation. Flexibility. Emphasis on individual accountability.	Fierce competition. Developing people for business expansion. New services. Maintaining position in market.	Intensively competitive markets. Enhancing product quality. Further market penetration. Continuing to change practices and attitudes.	To establish free-standing experience sharing networks to replace the LCP.

elements within each example which interest you. Compare your notes with the Code of CD practice and consider ways in which the organizations can further develop CD. Consider the implications for developing CD in your own organization. (The Prompt Lists in Chapter Five may help you.)

1 The Soap and Detergent Industry Association
Continuous development within an industry association

1 Background data

1.1 *Composition*

The Soap and Detergent Industry Association is an independent Trade Association of over 60 member companies – large, medium and small, including names such as Lever Brothers, Procter and Gamble, Colgate-Palmolive, Cussons and Yardley. Their common interest is hygiene and cleanliness, since each is involved in marketing, making, packaging, or supplying raw materials for soap and detergent products.

The industry is responsible for producing some one and a quarter million tonnes per annum of finished soaps and detergents of all types; the total sales volume has shown steady growth over the past ten years. Productivity has also steadily improved. A feature of the industry is the level of competitive activity between SDIA member firms, which has produced much innovation in terms of both technical products and marketing methods. Current man-power is approximately 13,500 of whom about 13% are managers above supervisory level.

The controlling body of the SDIA is its Council of fifteen, which meets practically every month, on which the chief executives of the major companies, or heads of appropriate divisions, represent their organizations. Their meetings address primarily political, legal and consumerist issues that arise at industry level, together with internal matters brought to their attention by their sub-committees or individual members. Administrative support is supplied by a small full-time office staff, led by the full-time Director-General.

1.2   *The education and training function*

During the '60s and '70s, SDIA members were within
scope to the Chemical and Allied Products Industry
Training Board – indeed, CAPITB drew heavily on
several SDIA firms' expertise in creating its committees.
Whilst these firms initially supported the concept of the
national training body, they increasingly came to believe
that CAPITB offered little to SDIA members, and they
resented (a) the financial contributions they were called
upon to make, and (b) the increasingly bureaucratic
operation. Discussions in SDIA Council at the end of the
'70s turned simultaneously on the lack of respect for ITBs
and on the increasing importance of training to serve
specific growth, productivity and innovation aims. These
discussions led in 1981 – before the demise of CAPITB –
to the formation of SDIA's Education and Training
Committee, which has since operated alongside other
SDIA committees which cover technical, legal and safety
matters.

2   Policy/philosophy

The Education and Training Committee's initial Terms
of Reference included the following:

- to generally promote amongst SDIA members a
  recognition of the importance of continuing, job-
  related, situation-specific training at the workplace

- to keep under constant review the. . .industry's manpower requirements, especially with regard to
  identifiable skills, and to alert the industry whenever
  a serious shortage of skills seems likely, recommending strategy as necessary

- to keep under constant review external education
  and training facilities. . .and to advise SDIA
  members on appropriate facilities

> – to monitor and influence developments emanating from [national policy making and strategic bodies] and to provide advice on these developments . . . .

(SDIA – E & T Committee Terms of Reference, 1981)

Much of the early work of the committee hinged on definition of philosophy and strategy. At the end of the second year, the Chairman's annual report contained the following commentary:

> Basically, our philosophy aims at promoting 'continuous operational learning' – that is, activity which serves improved operational performance on the part of both the firm and the individual. Ideally, continuous operational learning is planned on a self-help basis – that is, unique decisions are taken at the workplace and the learning itself is integrated as closely as possible with the work itself.

(SDIA – E & T Committee Annual Report, 1983)

These ideas have been regularly restated to members through E & T Notes, annual reports and strategic papers. They have been consistently approved by the Council, and appear to have the support of member firms. A recent strategic paper notes:

> The fundamental philosophy is of self-help aimed at promoting 'continuous development' – that is, activity which continuously seeks to improve operational learning on the part of both firm and individual by identifying training needs and developing appropriate responses. The job of both the SDIA Council and its Training Committee is to stimulate learning initiatives, to develop understanding of learning processes, and to provide up to date guidance on resources that might help. Collective action and funding is only envisaged when it is clear that the necessary resources are unavailable elsewhere.

(SDIA – 'Key Issues Relating to Training Strategy', 1986)

3   Continuous development practice

3.1   *Responsibilities and roles*

The E & T Committee has to date been composed of Personnel and Training management from major SDIA member firms, plus a few line managers from small companies (eg a Managing Director who also chairs a Youth Training operation), a Training Adviser (who is retained on a part-time basis) and the full-time SDIA Director-General, who acts as Secretary to all SDIA committees. They meet formally at least quarterly, but much work is completed outside formal meetings, the Chairman, Director-General, and Training Adviser being in continuous contact.

Expenses incurred by those members of SDIA committees who are employed by member firms are not charged to SDIA; they are carried by the employing organizations. This is in keeping with the view that these are properly borne as operating expenses and recovered in the price of the products.

A typical E & T Committee meeting agenda will contain items on:

(a) external developments, such as MSC initiatives
(b) news from sister associations such as the Chemical Industries Association or the Food Manufacturers Federation, and
(c) internal matters such as the SDIA Soapmaking Course.

Visitors often attend by invitation – the MSC contact regularly visits, and it is normal to invite someone who can discuss with first-hand knowledge an agenda item (eg multi-skills training).

As implied above, the prime job of both SDIA Council and its E & T Committee is to stimulate developments which serve its philosophy and objectives. To that end, Council receives a verbal report from the E & T Committee at each of its meetings; the E & T Chairman attends as required, but the Director-General normally acts as the communicator. The report typically offers strategic advice, together with proposals for specific actions. Council discussions have covered a wide range of issues – from responses to government white papers on the future of industrial training and MSC initiatives (eg on youth and adult training), to proposals stemming from internal questionnaires.

Ways in which non-involved bodies might contribute to SDIA members' improved business performance have often been discussed within the E & T Committee. This issue is a complex one: essentially a trade association and not an employers' federation, SDIA does not have any particular local base, nor any strong connection with a particular education authority. There is no obvious focal trade union point with which it would be appropriate for SDIA to work. The view taken has been that it is best for each SDIA member to establish its own links with those external bodies which are relevant to its own needs – and indeed that this flexible approach will contribute best to operational success.

3.2 *Identification of learning opportunities and needs*

The self-help philosophy assumes that each SDIA member will, on a continuing basis, determine learning needs which are specific to actual operational needs.

> . . .imposed national practices or standards are not favoured, and collective levies are seen as counter-productive. The. . .SDIA role is to provide an intelligence service for members, enabling them to mount specific training activities which serve their own competitive needs.
>
> (SDIA – 'Key Issues Relating to Training Strategy', 1986)

To encourage this, E & T Notes – compiled by the Training Adviser on a monthly basis – carry to members the results of Council and E & T Committee discussions, plus a commentary on current national developments and information on newly appearing resources. E & T Notes are distributed to all members with Council minutes. Special appendices are issued from time to time: subjects such as Industry Year, YTS regulations, and safety training resources have been dealt with in this way.

Special strategic papers have addressed likely future priorities – both in terms of training content and training methods. These have explored trends in employment, in organizations, and in technology, outlining probable learning needs for all. One such paper – covering training methods under the headings of Management, Office Staff, Sales Forces and Factory Staff – used a 'Prompt List' approach, against which members could review their own situation to determine their own needs. The introductory paragraphs included the following:

It is perhaps worth stressing that few of the Prompt List items assume formal off-the-job lecture-type courses as the standard training opportunity. In many ways, organizational learning can be promoted via organizational instruments, with employees naturally acquiring new knowledge/understanding as part of their day to day work. This is an ideal to which SDIA aspires: the integration of training and work as part of the ongoing, day to day operational reality.

(SDIA – 'Training Methods in a Changing Climate', 1983)

Periodic questionnaires have asked members to notify the Director-General of training needs which the member cannot satisfy. Subjects such as computer technology, abrasive wheels and soapmaking (see 3.4 below) have emerged; most have been easily dealt with by finding appropriate external resources. The Training Adviser maintains information on a wide range of external resources; he is also available to members on request as a 'free consultant'.

SDIA has not taken a stance on 'systematic' devices such as job descriptions and specifications, nor again on appraisal schemes – although it is known that most members use such organizational instruments. It has been regularly stated that members should determine for themselves the relevance of these instruments to their own operations, should review their value periodically, and should not allow such instruments to undermine the employee's responsibility for self development.

3.3 *Learner involvement*

Strategic papers have emphasized the increasing importance of employee participation and involvement, and the evolution of more 'open' work systems. Those addressing training methods have also stressed that the motivation to learn is a critical prerequisite for individual learning in the continuous development culture, and that consultation with potential learners is a way to promote that motivation through 'ownership' of training plans.

One strategic paper has explicitly covered employee participation and involvement from a training point of view:

The Training Committee recognizes both employee participation and involvement as being essential elements in the achievement of company objectives – and takes the view that they can be managed well or indifferently, with corresponding effects on business results.
(SDIA – 'Employee Participation and Involvement', 1985)

This paper took as its framework the 1982 Employment Act – and in particular the four types of arrangement that should be reported in Directors' Reports. Against each, SDIA members were offered:

(a) a list of areas in which employee training might be needed
(b) a Prompt List for senior managers to review current practice

(c) suggested source material for trainers.

The approach was not prescriptive; the aim was essentially to help members create their own plans by involving them in a review of their practice against the emerging legislation.

3.4   *Learning resources*

Whilst free advice is available and frequent stimuli are offered, members are expected to create or buy their own learning resources, treating the expense as a normal operating one; only in exceptional circumstances will SDIA consider providing a direct training facility. This has however been done with the Soapmaking Course – which offers low cost basic instruction in the processes of soapmaking and packaging, and is not available elsewhere. The course brings together technical experts who either work within or have recently retired from the industry, and who pass on basic technology to nominated newcomers – often graduate trainees who have no previous knowledge of soapmaking chemistry or engineering. The E & T Committee is currently exploring the viability of reproducing this course, with its structured handouts, in a 'distance learning' form – thus providing the opportunity for it to be studied by individuals on a self-help basis.

SDIA have also assisted companies wanting to take advantage of MSC grant-aid opportunities, where MSC insist on grant claims being processed at industry level.

E & T Notes contain much information on learning resources. One of the Training Adviser's duties is to keep up to date with learning methods, and especially the application to learning of new technology; useful sources of data to this end have been 'Training Digest' (obtained by SDIA on a subscription basis and distributed to all E & T Committee members) and 'New Technologies in Training' conferences. Close watch is kept on products emerging from such bodies as the Industrial Training Research Unit, the National Foundation for Educational Research, and the Institute of Personnel Management.

The IPM Code of Practice on Continuous Development has been distributed throughout the industry, and a pamphlet, 'Learn how to Learn' (created by the now defunct 'Training of Trainers Advisory Group'), was given to members as an insert in the strategic paper 'Training Methods in a Changing Climate'.

The general SDIA view remains that of self-help, however. It is assumed and recommended that management within member firms create the environment in which continuous development can prosper by endlessly searching for improved performance and mounting learning activity to that end. This is seen as *the* critical resource – the commitment of management to continous development:

> Managers will increasingly be faced with problems they have not encountered before. . .skills which will be at a premium , and which will be conspicuous by their absence if they do not exist, are OBSERVATION skills, ANALYSIS skills and DECISION skills. Other important skill needs will relate to COMMUNICA-TION. . .to COUNSELLING, to PROMOTING TEAMWORK; straightforward knowledge of these skills will not be sufficient to manage the essential human development which the ever-changing environment demands. . .It will be necessary for management teams to explore within their own work the extent to which [new concepts and instruments set out elsewhere in the paper] apply to them.
>
> (SDIA – 'Key Issues Relating to Training Strategy', 1986)

4   Problems

Internally, few problems have been encountered other than those (for example, of communication) encountered in the management of any dynamic operation. The SDIA Council has rarely differed from the E & T Committee in its strategic or philosophical stance; the E & T Committee itself has been consistently collective in decisions, and consensus has been easy to reach.

Apart from the monthly E & T Notes, every publication that will be seen by the outside world is agreed in both E & T Committee and Council. Inevitably, the contents carry different implications for different readers; considerable time and effort has been spent in 'polishing' publications so that views are not compromised. It is also normal for documents addressed to members to carry an explicit statement that the contents offer guidance and in no way commit the individual member to its adoption.

SDIA's dialogue with MSC has often been characterized by differing views on how SDIA should organize and/or influence its members; some MSC decisions have seemed to challenge SDIA's self-help philosophy and to assume dependancy on the part of SDIA members (although others have suggested the reverse). The same has been true of opinions voiced by representatives of other non-statutory training organizations, who have suggested (for example, in the CBI's panel of Non-Statutory Training Organizations representatives, which SDIA regularly attends) that their role is best managed in a prescriptive framework. The SDIA answer to this has been to engage in discussion on the subject, and to publicize its views, whenever and wherever possible; but it has not been suggested that the SDIA model will be appropriate for all industrial training organizations. The E & T Committee has been pleased to find that a 1986 MSC publication, 'The Effective NSTO', appears to support the SDIA model as one of a number of possible routes to a common end.

5 Results and achievements

The achievements have been significant.

- General acceptance within the industry of the importance of learning strategy, learning systems and learning activities. Whilst this remains an uncompleted task – and is likely to remain so for a long time – the signs are that chief executives in most, if not all, SDIA member firms acknowledge the importance of learning at the workplace.

- Similarly an adherence to the continuous development philosophy; improved performance and improved commercial results are – within the competitive framework – key industry and member goals on an endless basis.

- Relatively few skills shortages. Periodic reviews have shown up few areas in which members give manpower shortages as a reason for failure to achieve operational ends. The practice of 'growing one's own resources' is itself growing, and whilst well-trained staff are sometimes lost to predators, there are usually successors in the pipeline. The exceptions – in engineering and computer skills – are seen by SDIA as reflecting a national shortage of adequate material emerging from higher education.

- Contribution to national initiatives – such as Industry Year and the Youth Training Scheme – have been quick and substantial. The SDIA's Training Adviser has been involved in projects mounted by the CBI, the IPM, the DES and the MSC: he and other E & T Committee members have served on a variety of external bodies.

- Commercial results. The industry has a record second to none in terms of 'improved value for the customer'. The price of products is significantly below that obtaining in other EC countries; new technology has been introduced and product improvements have appeared with great frequency throughout the difficult years of the '70s and '80s; and productivity improvement has been continuous.

2   The Civil Service/Cabinet Office
Continuous management development within the Civil Service

1   Background data

There are well over 22,000 managers within the Civil Service. Responsibility for co-ordinating and developing a continuous, structured approach to the training and development of staff rests with the Management and Personnel Office of the Cabinet Office, and more particularly with its Training Division.

During the '70s and early '80s, the core of management development activity for Civil Service managers comprised varied job experience and succession planning, complemented by attendance at relevant Civil Service College and other external programmes. It was possible however for people of high potential to go through the important middle career years – from the late 20s to the early 40s – with very little planned training. Precisely what the organization might need of these managers in terms of knowledge, abilities and skills was not spelled out anywhere – and by the early '80s it was becoming increasingly accepted that those very things were themselves changing through time.

2   Policy/philosophy

Cabinet Office discussions focused on the need for a long-term approach to the development of senior managers, and one which could marry the principles of continuous development with varied job experience. Training decisions needed to address 'improved managerial competence' aims as well as placement plans, and such decisions had to be owned more consciously by the people who were being developed. The principles set out in the Institute of Personnel Management's Code 'Continuous Development: People and Work' – continuous learning, the integration of learning with work, self development, and the promotion of learning resources – were seen to be relevant, significant and worthy of implementation.

Early in 1984, a Director was appointed to establish a new Top Management Programme – a six-week developmental course for staff newly appointed to the very senior grade of Under Secretary. (The course, which now runs some four times a year and is probably the most senior programme run by anyone on a regular basis in the UK, includes an equal number of Civil Service personnel and top managers from outside the Service.) The plans for the Top Management Programme focused attention on the need for more systematic improvement of arrangements for the training and development of staff in grades immediately below that of Under Secretary; accordingly, the Head of Training Division (Mr Peter Coster) was commissioned to undertake a study and make proposals. This led to the Coster Report of May 1984.

The Coster Report recommended that:

- a senior management development programme should be set up to supply 'a structured approach to training and development'

- the programme should be for senior staff between the grades of Principal and Assistant Secretary, and should cover specialists (eg engineers, lawyers) as well as administrators

- the twin aims should be better preparation for future senior managers, and greater effectiveness in current grades regardless of whether they were likely to reach more senior levels

- there should be a strong element of individual responsibility and self-help, but individuals should be offered help to plan their personal development

- a minimum 'annual training target' of 5 days per participant should be set at the start

- research should be undertaken to establish what competences the Civil Service wanted these staff to have

- initial concentration should be on about 3,500 'younger staff' from the 22,000 in the relevant grades

- overt top management commitment was essential.

These recommendations were quickly accepted, and Training Division was asked to see that the new Senior Management Development Programme was designed and implemented in all major government departments by September 1985.

3   Continuous development practice

3.1   *Responsibilities and roles*

Training Division, Cabinet Office (Management and
Personnel Office) were responsible, in consultation with
individual departments for drawing up the framework of
the Senior Management Development Programme, for
designing documentation, and for marketing the
Programme. They have subsequently provided advice to
departments, and have monitored and evaluated progress,
developing and refining the Programme as necessary.
Within departments:

Top Management have had to demonstrate their continuing commitment to the success of the Programme,
and to communicate this support to staff by means, for
example, of personal invitations to participate; public
reference to the Programme; or the request of departmental progress reports.

Management have been responsible for discussing and
reviewing with participants the latter's personal
development plans, and providing relevant advice and
guidance. Each participant has been assigned to a
senior colleague (normally the line manager) for this
purpose.

Departmental Personnel and Training Divisions have
been responsible for providing expert advice and information to both participants and line managers on
particular aspects of development such as training
opportunities and jobs. The precise spread of responsibilities between the two divisions has varied, depending
upon which government department is involved. A
particular responsibility of Personnel Divisions has
been to foster the integrative aspects of the Programme,
and to use it – and the information it generates – as a
means of more effectively matching people to jobs
(for both current operational and developmental
purposes).

3.2 *Identification of learning opportunities and needs*

Research into 'what senior managers need to be good at' had four strands:

(a) existing knowledge and data
(b) work already done for the Top Management Programme
(c) a survey by questionnaire of potential participants, which produced an 80% response from a sample of 530. The approach was to present a long list of activities and to ask respondents to score each activity which formed a part of the 'present job', for both 'importance' and 'difficulty'. Questions were also asked about 'knowledge needed' but no direct replies on 'training needs' were sought
(d) a series of structured interviews with top management, who were asked to contribute their views on what their staff needed to be good at, and how it was likely to change through time.

From this data, shortlists of competences were drawn up:

A. 'Core' Competences – likely to be needed in ALL occupations:

- management of resources/organizations
- management of staff
- knowledge/understanding of your work context
- 'managing your own work'
- information technology
- more specialized knowledge/expertise.

(NB Each of these items carried detailed sub-headings.)

B. 'Important' Competences – not universally needed, but important where the need exists:

- representational/presentational skills
- written/administrative skills
- policy management

- economics
- accounting and finance
- quantitative skills/statistics
- law
- industrial relations.

These lists of competences form the heart of the key Senior Management Development Programme working document, the 'Personal Development Plan'.

The Personal Development Plan gives the learner a description of the learning system, plus a structure from which he/she can assess, plan and review. In its early paragraphs, it explains the roles the learner and his senior colleague ('your Manager') are expected to play; it explains the concept of 'competences', and how competences can be developed in a variety of ways. Each competence is listed; against each, the learner is asked to record what he/she has already learned – from experience or formal training – and whether it is important to develop it further.

3.3   *Learner involvement*

The Senior Management Development Programme has not been imposed on managers. Invitations to join were sent out by the Permanent Secretary, accompanied by an attractive leaflet. Introductory meetings and seminars were held for those who wanted to know more. 77% of the 3,500 invited opted in during the first 6 months, and more have joined since.

A major point, stressed to all, is that the Personal Development Plan is 'owned' throughout by the participant. After its initial completion, it is discussed and agreed with the learner's manager; the discussion follows the Personal Development Plan format in leading to:

(a) the most important *objective* for development
(b) a *plan* for development over the next year
(c) *suggestions* for development over the next three years.

It has also been stressed that learners are not expected to strive for 'ticks against headings'; nor are the competences to be seen as strait-jackets. They are intended to serve as a frame of reference to enable the learner and the superior to create practical, work-related development plans. An example of a work-related development plan (reprinted in the Personal Development Plan itself) is:

Date of Plan .... Year Ends: December ....

- Visit each Division in my dept with whose finances I deal
- Go through self-instruction package on Govt accounting
- Attend training course on Public Expenditure White Paper at Civil Service College on ....

At the end of a given year, the process is completed by an end-of-year review involving both learner and manager and enabling the learner to roll the whole thing forward via another 'assess, plan, review' cycle.

3.4 Learning resources

The Cabinet Office has already produced an extensive catalogue of Civil Service College courses, and information is also circulated on a wide range of external training resources. It is hoped that through time a battery of self-study materials (similar to that named in the example above, which has been specially produced by Training Division) will be made available.

4 Problems

Although the Senior Management Development Programme was created and launched by the target date, completion of the Personal Development Plans has been rather slow: about one third of the participants had Personal Development Plans completed in the first six months, the remainder taking a further six months. It seems that both learners and superiors need to get used to the system, and especially the amount of time required to produce something worthwhile.

There has of course been some scepticism. Individuals have shown concern that once needs are identified and plans drawn up, management may not provide the resources (including time) necessary to bring them to fruition. The setting of the 5-day training target has inevitably created stresses at a time of resource constraint.

It is also clear that the Senior Management Development Programme, with its strong emphasis on self-help and self development calls for a change in some attitudes towards training and development. Too many managers still expect things to be done for them when it is they who should take the initiative.

Another key need is for top management and Training Division to keep up the enthusiasm and create ways whereby departments can increase the support available for 'the managers of learners'.

5   Results and achievements

A first survey of the impact of the new programme was made in five departments some twelve months after it was begun; it involved discussions with groups of participants (without their managers present) and separate subsequent discussions with those responsible for implementation. The survey covered only about 50 participants, but produced much data on the issues involved in establishing the scheme, and pointers to future priorities.

Virtually everyone believed that the individual planning process and the use of the Personal Development Plan was valuable. Participants welcomed the rigour and discipline inherent in the approach, and felt that valuable knowledge was gained merely by involving oneself in the process. One department had 'discovered' such a high degree of concern with industrial relations issues that a series of special briefings had been arranged. Another department experienced interest among high flyers in 'doing a management job to round out their experience'; the department felt that the use of the Personal Development Plan was likely to be a useful counter-balance to expediency in job postings. The latter department had added to the system by instituting, as standard practice, a structured interview with the Personnel Manager after the Personal Development Plan was first completed.

The survey has pointed to areas which require concentration of effort. These include marketing and presentation; continuing top management interest; the role of line managers; links with current staff appraisal procedures; the role of personnel management; advice on self development; and continued advice and support on career development.

Basic statistical data have been collected, and an annual update enquiry is to be instituted. This will cover:

- numbers of newly eligible staff opting into the Programme
- numbers dropping out of the Programme, with details of reasons
- numbers of participants at the year end
- numbers completing a Personal Development Plan during the year
- percentage of participants who do not complete 5 days' training in a year
- departmental views on achievements/ideas for improvements.

As mentioned in 4 above, Training Division and top management have learned lessons related to the move from dependency to self development. It is also clear that the basic system – and especially its assumptions on competences – need to be constantly reviewed and updated; a mini-review took place in 1987 (two years into the initiative), and a more substantial review is likely at the five-year mark. Decisions will also be taken on extending the system to take in larger numbers – albeit still on a voluntary basis.

But to have launched the Senior Management Development Programme has itself been a major achievement, and to obtain the early, active involvement of so many people suggests that:

- the introduction of a continuous development approach is welcomed by the learners
- the voluntary approach is necessary to secure the considerable commitment required to participate
- it is possible to produce a tailor-made system which can integrate personal development plans with work priorities and corporate plans for varied job experience.

The Senior Management Development Programme is not merely a continuous process of learning and development for the participants: the aim is that it should become a fundamental part of the ongoing management system.

3   West Bromwich Building Society
Continuous development within a building society

1   Background data

West Bromwich Building Society is the twenty-fifth largest building society in the UK, with assets approaching £500 million and a network of some 80 branches, mainly in the Midlands and Wales. Expansion during the past decade has involved the creation of a new Chief Office block, the development of computerized operations, and a marked increase in the rate of operational change.

Employees currently number 500, of whom about 100 are managers. With the possible exception of a few Chief Office jobs, work at all levels involves significant contact with 'users', that is, Society members with investments and/or mortgages. Services offered to users have extended and become more sophisticated during recent years; this process will further accelerate with the advent of new legislation (which has freed the societies from former restrictions and allows them to compete with the clearing banks by offering a much wider range of services). So – operational development and employee learning have been recognized by top management for some time as continuing and interrelated needs.

As the Society's work has increased in complexity, so staff have been encouraged to contribute to improving procedures and methods. The introduction of computerized operations, for example, gave a much-needed opportunity for staff in Branch offices, and again for elected Staff Association members, to influence what was introduced to deal with new-style counter dealing.

2   Policy/philosophy

The '80s have seen the clarification of a battery of 'employment policies', and the publication of statements for employees on such subjects as manpower planning, recruitment and selection, health and safety, equal opportunities, work organization and training. The last-named statement contains the following:

> It is expected that all staff will avail themselves of the training opportunities available both internally and externally.
>
> Moreover, everyone should strive to improve performance by using each new experience as a vehicle for developing skills and knowledge. The practice of this continuous learning process is to be encouraged at all levels of staff throughout the Society. . .
>
> It is the responsibility of all Managers to ensure the continued development of their staff through planned training. . . . In the first instance, Managers are expected to train their own staff. This 'on-the-job' training must be supplemented by the use of other training resources. . . .
>
> In addition to training, the Society actively encourages staff to study for relevant professional qualifications. Provisions have been made to assist with time off for study and to meet the cost of fees. . .the Society expects career staff to contribute considerable personal resources to self development, in recognition of the

facilities provided by the Society. . . .
(West Bromwich Building Society, 'Employment Policies', August 1985)

The emphasis on 'improved performance', and management's responsibility to make subordinates aware of *their* responsibility to promote continuous development, have increasingly been stressed during the '80s.

Management resourcing policy has been established on a 'homegrown' basis. Staff can be listed as 'management trainees' following appraisal and management recommendation; all staff are encouraged to obtain appropriate professional qualifications. Top management have traditionally been active in serving the Chartered Building Societies Institute, especially in relation to local branches.

3   Continuous development practice

3.1   *Responsibilities and roles*

While the Chief Office organization includes a central training unit (see below), the prime responsibility rests with line management – notably the 80 Branch Managers and a small team of Area Managers. The following describes the basic organization:

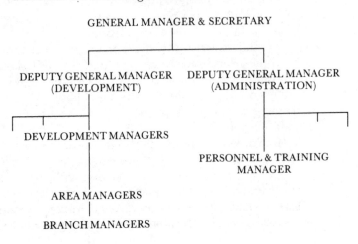

The roving Area Managers bring together responsibility for (a) business development (eg Marketing) and (b) Personnel and Administration development. They constantly monitor reality, and stimulate operational change, either in line with corporate plans or against perceived opportunities. Discussions on 'improved performance' with Branch Managers often include the creation of Branch or individual learning plans. If and when central resources are needed, the Central Training Unit is brought in; but much of the development is implemented by the Branch Managers on their own initiative. Branch Managers have available the facility of a weekly 'training session' (Tuesday morning – see 3.4 below) which is routinely used for communicating new information to staff and for refresher training. Branch Managers are also responsible for the induction of new staff, and for ongoing coaching as needed.

The Management Appraisal Form (see 3.3 below) contains the following question under the heading 'Training and Development':

How much time does jobholder spend training, coaching, developing himself and staff? Does jobholder discuss these matters with staff other than at Appraisal times? Are pre- and post-course briefings executed?

(West Bromwich Building Society, 'Management Appraisal Form')

The central Personnel and Training unit has four roles:

(a) to make staff (especially managers) aware – on a continuous basis – of the need for all to carry responsibility for their own development

(b) to stimulate an appropriate environment and provide adequate resources

(c) to help with specific training problems

(d) to devise, create and administer a menu of central training courses.

Success is monitored and judged by top management, subjectively, on a continuous basis. Overall strategy and system development originate at top level, ongoing responsibility resting with the Deputy General Manager (Administration); if and when a major strategic development is introduced (eg new Information Technology), it appears as part of the annual corporate plan – which is communicated in full to all employees.

3.2   *Identification of learning opportunities and needs*

An annual Training Plan and Budget is drafted by the central Personnel and Training unit after consideration of:

(a) the annual corporate plan

(b) review of past training activity

(c) discussions with key managers, eliciting the latters' views on priorities for improved performance

(NB: It is expected that in the future a questionnaire will be introduced to allow ALL managers to give their views on training priorities for the 2-year period ahead.)

(d) appraisal and assessment data (see 3.3 below)

(e) outputs from special reviews/projects (see 4 below).

The recommended plan is presented to top management, who amend and authorize accordingly. This influences later ad hoc management discussions; it also acts as the blueprint for what the Chief Office provides in courses and resources.

It should not be forgotten that mainstream 'continuous development' activity – which inevitably involves the identification of learning needs and opportunities at the workplace – stems from the ongoing dialogue between management, and again between managers and other staff, in the Branch Offices. Whilst this dialogue takes place within the context of existing operational and training plans, it additionally serves operational problems and opportunities as they occur at the workplace. Much of the resulting development activity is not termed 'training'; it is simply 'ongoing work activity'.

3.3 *Learner involvement*

As already noted, discussions on performance are expected to be held regularly throughout any given year; more formal appraisal activity is required annually. Forms are distributed by the central Personnel and Training unit for this purpose; the operation is staggered throughout the year to allow adequate time to be spent on the task.

Separate appraisal forms exist for managers and for those below management level. The latter form lists seven factors (including Accuracy, Speed, Accceptance of Responsibility, Relations with Staff/Public), against each of which a rating must be given from a 4-point scale. The appraisor:

> must comment on those areas of performance where the assessment is 'C' or 'D' – (in spite of the fact that 'C' is labelled 'Satisfactory') – detailing plans for improvement, eg training courses, coaching, counselling, setting of targets. . .

> (West Bromwich Building Society, 'Staff Appraisal Form')

The Management Appraisal Form is more comprehensive, requiring detailed comments against a battery of specific questions (including that on Training and Development quoted in 3.1 above) under three general headings of 'Planning, Controlling and Organizing', 'People', and 'Communication'. Depending upon what is entered on the appraisal form, subsidiary forms are completed at interview and list key objectives, skills development aims, together with action plans for the future. Appraisees at all levels are party to whatever appears on these forms.

A significant input to appraisal discussions is another form – the 'Self Assessment Form' – which is distributed along with the appraisal forms. Appraisees can choose whether they wish to use this form or not: increasingly they complete them before formal interviews take place, the information on them providing a key input to the discussions. The eight questions on the Self Assessment Form are:

(1) What do you consider to be your strong points in the job?

(2) What have you accomplished of particular note since your last Appraisal?

(3) Is there anything you would like your Manager to clarify about your job, Society policy, departmental activities?

(4) Have you any suggestions for improving work practices?

(5) Is your present job in line with the sort of career pattern that suits you? (Give reasons in either case, and show your preferred pattern.)

(6) Would you appreciate the type of career pattern which would give you a change from time to time, even if no promotion was involved?

(7) Are there any points about your work, ambitions or interests which affect the course your career might take?

(8) What training and development would you welcome from the point of view of –
   (a) your present job?
   (b) possible future jobs?
   (c) general.

(West Bromwich Building Society, 'Self Assessment Form')

All appraisal and self assessment forms are sent to the central Personnel and Training unit when completed; they are however returned to the relevant line managers once the data is centrally collated. As already implied, they influence both central training plans and ongoing learning at the workplace – especially that which the Branch Manager arranges.

3.4 *Learning resources*

The most significant learning resource is time: organizational decisions have been taken with this in mind, managers in particular being used as coaches, counsellors, instructors and briefers. The ever-increasing need to communicate new information, and the growth of defined learning needs, have led to the imposition of a 'Training Period' in Branch Officers – pre 9.30 am on Tuesday mornings.

Beyond this, professional study leave is granted wherever appropriate; internal course facilities are continuously reviewed and extended as necessary; external specialists are provided where they do not exist internally, and external courses similarly patronized; and self-study materials are beginning to be used. It is likely that one of the Society's major future training developments will be the introduction of computer-assisted learning programmes, which could replace traditional lectures and information sessions as mainstream resources.

4 Problems

It would be wrong to suggest that the CD style and culture have evolved without problems, or to suggest that the development is complete.

Whilst the general mood within the Society has been supportive, and top management have given a strong lead, some managers have themselves been reticent to promote their own CD approaches. Some have at times insisted that they 'cannot manage the training function without more help', or that they 'don't know how to train'. Hence training skills – instruction, coaching, counselling, interviewing – now loom large in central management course objectives. And the Tuesday training sessions, use of which has been 'somewhat patchy', offer regular opportunities to practise skills and generate confidence.

Specific operational problems are often addressed by the creation of special cross-functional working parties. At the time this case example was being researched, a 12-person group (comprising staff from various departments and levels, and including the head of Personnel and Training) was engaged on a review of internal 'communications'. Following early briefing and objective-setting meetings, a whole-day, off-site session produced a set of recommendations for top management to judge.

5   Results and achievements

The overall achievement is the establishment of a 'continuous learning' system, and the acceptance of 'improved performance' as *the* ongoing aim for all levels and types of staff. This system itself must be maintained – and the attitude constantly renewed – as a normal part of the Society's business; but experience during the '80s suggests that it is increasingly valued by staff, and commercial results to date provide the necessary incentive for further CD moves.

From a long list of possible 'lessons learned', the following seem to be most significant:

- developing a CD culture takes a long time

- CD is not something that people naturally identify with, but it *is* appreciated when offered

- self development has to be encouraged with time and finance for all except the most highly motivated staff

- CD must be accompanied by salary and job progression if it is to be seen as meaningful in employees' eyes.

As already noted, 1986 saw the start of a new era for building societies, with a wide range of new business operations becoming legally viable options. As West Bromwich Building Society introduces new activities, so the CD system identifies and manages the learning that accrues.

Separately, to give greater skills to the top fifteen managers (the Executive plus 12 heads of department), an intensive tailor-made course has been introduced. This represents a development from an earlier management skills course, and is an example of newly defined 'improved performance' aims being reflected in training plans and learning activity. The investigation into internal communications mentioned above is expected similarly to identify a range of learning priorities.

In addition to the system developments already suggested, the Society may introduce a manpower planning element into its forward planning activity. The appearance of an IT strategy is likely to bring with it a need for some specialist recruitment, plus a major programme of internal training at all levels.

The CD system itself will of course be continuously monitored and developed.

4 Nabisco Group Limited
Continuous development in managing food manufacturing and selling operations

1 Background data

Nabisco Group Limited is one of the UK's leading food companies. It is the country's leading supplier of snacks through its Smiths and Walker brands; in biscuits, with brand names including Jacobs Club, Cream Cracker, Ritz, Twiglets, it enjoys a fifth of the market; and its breakfast cereals (Shredded Wheat and others), hold third place. Its annual turnover is in excess of £500 million. Some 12,000 staff – about 650 of whom are managers – operate from 20 factory and office locations.

The company has experienced dramatic changes since 1982, when it acquired the much larger Huntley and Palmer Foods plc, and more recently as a result of the 1985 merger of its parent company, Nabisco Brands Inc of New Jersey, USA, with R J Reynolds Inc of Winston Salem, North Carolina, USA. The first of these developments produced a UK organization with a wide variety of traditions, cultures, policies and practices; in 1983 it was seen by a newly established top management team as 'disparate and underperforming'.

The company's annual report at the end of 1983 said:

> Much. . .remains to be done. [Planned improvements] include upgrading the UK biscuit production to be at least the equal of the best in the industry, both in terms of efficiency and product quality; further improving the efficiency of the distribution network; mounting an aggressive new product development programme. . . .
> (Nabisco Brands Ltd 'Report and Accounts, 1983')

1984 saw the inception of a wide variety of initiatives in Nabisco's Personnel operations, complementing those in the technical, marketing, distribution and commercial fields. New policies were formulated, new systems introduced, new industrial relations agreements reached, new senior management appointments made, and so on.

This case example explains the way in which, as part of its revitalization programme, Nabisco introduced 'continuous development' (CD) processes into its management operation.

2   Policy/philosophy

Nabisco has not to date used the precise term 'continuous development' in its approach to improving management performance, but CD principles have been at the heart of initiatives which were concerned with 'Performance Management'.

With the aid of HAY-MSL consultants, the Nabisco Director of Human Resource Planning and Development completed a series of structured interviews with key managers across the organization – the aims being to clarify the context within which management might become a more consistent process whilst acknowledging the differing operational needs of the various business Divisions. Particular attention was paid to current practices which addressed links between performance appraisal and salary rewards. Managers' views were sought on both 'present reality' and 'future improvement'.

Summarized findings were as follows:

- the wide variety of past practice was confirmed

- the wide range of current skills and styles was also confirmed, and defended by many

- polarized views existed on the desirability of establishing close links between performance appraisal and pay

- all wanted simplicity in whatever schemes were to be introduced

- all feared 'central impositions'

- there was general support for a scheme which would aim at improving management performance.

(From 'Management Grading, Performance Appraisal and Remuneration and Benefits Policy', Nabisco Group Ltd, 1983)

Policy Committee level discussions led to the decision to introduce a system of 'Performance Management'. The explicit 'mission aims' were:

(a) to ensure that [Nabisco] consistently develops and retains professional and management people whose abilities and experience are appropriate to its operational needs, and

(b) to ensure that our professional and management people find Nabisco a challenging organization in which to work, grow and stay.

('Human Resource Planning and Development', Nabisco 1984)

Behind these aims lay top management's intent to transform the Nabisco culture from one which was characterized by low pay and low productivity (at all levels) into one of 'high performance, high reward'.

3   Continuous development practice

The new strategy had four parts:

1. Measurement of performance
2. Clarification of roles and responsibilities
3. Linking of reward to performance
4. Improvements in levels of performance.

The second of these (NB: *not* covered in detail in this document), achieved with the aid of HAY-MSL consultants and using a HAY-MSL approach, provided a new framework for describing management jobs and abolished many inequities in salary and benefit practices. The process was completed in four months, and covered all levels of management from 'first level', upwards. The new system, and its effect on each individual, was communicated to individuals through individual briefings backed up with briefing documentation. Special 'job description seminars' were mounted for the 70 senior management members who had to lead the implementation process. An appeals procedure was established and Divisional grading panels constituted to deal with emerging problems.

The other elements were addressed through the introduction of a continuous 'Planning and Assessing Results' (PAR) system. The system is summarized as follows:

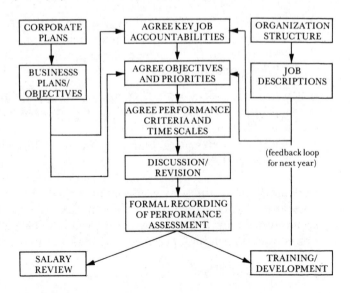

PAR was introduced 'top downwards', that is, the most senior management practised it before introducing it at the 'next level'. The pace of the development was left to Divisional management's discretion, with some departments outstripping others in the speed with which new procedures and processes were evolved and were introduced – and indeed improving significantly upon initial plans by the Board and Group Personnel.

3.1 Responsibilities and roles

As explained above, the *Nabisco Board* created, owned and at all times endorsed 'Performance Management' policy and strategy. *Board members and top divisional management* played key parts in introducing the new system and explaining its concepts in the early, formative period.

The *Director of Human Resource Planning and Development* has had overall responsibility for ensuring the ongoing evolution of the system and for monitoring and reporting on progress. The unit provided (and still provides) a considerable amount of advice to management in general. Guidance documents have set out to management what *must* be achieved in terms of outputs (for example, at least one formal appraisal must be completed each year), together with examples of forms and routines that might be adopted.

Line management have been encouraged to devise their own specific conventions within this system, the prime implementation role resting with senior management in the Divisions. This has ensured that what has been introduced (for example, a redesigned form) is *used*: the keynote is *flexibility*, with managers knowing that they are the owners of the detailed activity – that they can and must adapt detailed practice to serve their operational needs. Above all, *line management* are expected to operate the PAR system on a continuing basis, owning the *objectives and priorities* which the PAR system naturally produces, and managing the resulting training plans.

The *Group Personnel Director* was responsible for devising a new remuneration and benefits policy, incorporating a new rating system which was to be integrated with PAR to provide the the practical application of the 'high performance, high reward' philosophy.

3.2   *Identification of learning opportunities and needs*

Learning needs in Nabisco are now essentially viewed as 'objectives and criteria to promote the achievement of improved performance'. The process by which needs are identified is a discursive one, with the 'Outcomes' mandatory but the precise nature of the 'Steps' jointly determined by managers and their immediate superiors:

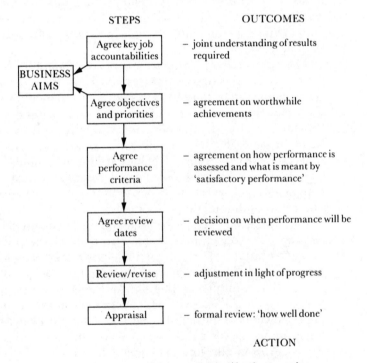

STEPS   OUTCOMES

Agree key job accountabilities   – joint understanding of results required

BUSINESS AIMS

Agree objectives and priorities   – agreement on worthwhile achievements

Agree performance criteria   – agreement on how performance is assessed and what is meant by 'satisfactory performance'

Agree review dates   – decision on when performance will be reviewed

Review/revise   – adjustment in light of progress

Appraisal   – formal review: 'how well done'

ACTION

– training/development plans

– salary review

Within this process, the concept of 'satisfactory performance' is an important one. It is *not* meant to imply 'minimum acceptable level', nor 'average level'; instead, it denotes the *norm* in a job which is being managed properly – a 'fully competent performance'.

3.3   *Learner involvement*

Since *agreed objectives* and *agreed performance criteria* are fundamental to PAR, the learner is fully involved in both the planning and the implementation processes. A key point in the original training of senior management was the stress placed on *joint* creation of objectives and performance criteria.

3.4   *Learning resources*

No special arrangements were made concerning learning resources. Learning needs which could only be satisfied by external activity (for example, courses) were collated by Personnel and Training units, and Divisional training budgets were created annually in line with priority needs endorsed by senior line management. Distance learning methods were not particularly sought after. Many learning needs were of course satisfied on a 'self development' basis without appearing anywhere in formal, collective lists of training needs. Managers were strongly encouraged to introduce at least one learning objective into each subordinate's set of objectives. (NB: Concurrently, another Nabisco initiative established new-style career development activities for selected managers, linked to a new succession planning system – the 'Career Planning Review' operation is not covered in this document.)

3.5   *The link with salaries*

As noted, a major corporate aim was to ensure that annual salary review properly reflected achievements in work performance. Five 'performance rating' levels were established, with that of 'Entirely Satisfactory Performance' as the mid-point (guidance documents provided lengthy and exhaustive definitions of each rating). Luckily, less than 5% of managers were in the top quartile of their current salary ranges: it was possible to re-define and streamline these ranges to fit with the new grading and rating structures, and at the same time to:

– permit flexibility in recruitment salaries
– provide scope for career development increases
– allow for promotions/demotions
– allow for increased responsibilities in a given grade, and
– (most importantly) reward improved performance.

Comprehensive briefing documentation was produced for each Division. Each manager was individually briefed by his/her line superior during January 1985, with managers' salaries the same month being moved to the minima of the new salary ranges.

Considerable effort by Group Personnel and senior management was put into helping the *joint* appraisal operation. Managers were advised how to prepare for formal interviews, and what those interviews should cover. Here are two checklists of points covered:

Problems Managers Face when Making Appraisals:

prejudice – like or dislike
halo or horn effect
too tought or too soft
too bland – central tendency
dislike of playing God
focus on last incident
personal style preferences
rate job size not performance
focus on part of job only
objectivity – rating on facts
unwillingness to risk conflict
not knowing their people.

Giving Feedback:

ask, don't tell
immediate is best
focus on performance *not* personality
focus on *his/her* performance
be specific and explain reasons
jointly analyse 'why'
positive and negative balance
key points only
actionable or need to know only
confront and explore differences
listen and be open to influence
keep it constructive
deal with points one at a time.

Staff were introduced to the PAR philosophy and system at a series of seminars in early 1985. The first PAR appraisals commenced in October 1985, PAR rating data being sent to Group Personnel a month later. New salaries were established and communicated to managers by Christmas, and were implemented in the January 1986 payroll. The annual sequence was (and is) as follows:

PERFORMANCE RATING
BY DIVISION
↓
Overall Rating
↓
Summary of Ratings
↓
Matrix
Generation ←— Rating
↓ ←— Salary Range
Salary Position on
Recommendations Scale
↓
Approval
↓
Salary Increase
and Payment

(NB: Bottom rating treated separately)

4   Problems

In the first full year of operation, the only substantial problem was the varying degrees of realism with which managers, including senior managers, established performance objectives and rated achievements.

Inevitably, standards varied between locations and departments; there was additionally a tendency for some senior managers to press for 'stretching' targets, with others holding out for less challenging goals. Paradoxically, there were instances where senior managers overrated performance, apparently feeling that their own performance ratings would suffer if their teams were not said to improve overall upon the 'Satisfactory' level.

This experience led Nabisco during 1986 to organize a number of 'Feedback and Training' meetings. These meetings concentrated on the underlying philosophy of 'Performance Management': considerable time was spent discussing the processes of objective setting and appraisal, and in particular the concept of 'Satisfactory' performance. Feedback from participants led to an appreciation of demotivating elements in the letters (A to D) used to describe performance levels – in particular, the 'C' rating was often interpreted wrongly as meaning 'average' or 'sub-standard'; a new set of titles has now been introduced which is expected to be both more descriptive and more motivating.

5   Results and achievements

It is difficult to report 'achievements' with real confidence against the small amount of experience to date. Nevertheless, top management are openly pleased about operational improvements during the period since 'Performance Management' was introduced. The 1985 Nabisco Group Review (published in 1986) reported a 'very satisfactory growth in turnover and profits', and went on:

> . . .accompanied by a parallel strengthening of management at all levels and by a further extension of our

modern and imaginative approach to employee relations.
(Nabisco Group Review, 1985)

Group Personnel Management believe that the devising
and introduction of no less than three new management
initiatives (Job Grading, Planning and Assessing Results,
and Salary Review) in such a short time – and coinciden-
tal with new industrial relations and productivity
developments for those below management level – has
been a major achievement. They also see 'Performance
Management' as a firm basis for long-term pride in the
company's operations, together with improved opportunities for personal growth.

5 IDOM (Ingenieria y Dirección de Obras y Montajes)
**Continuous development within a Spanish engineering
consultancy company**

1 Background data

IDOM (Ingenieria y Dirección de Obras y Montajes)
started to operate in 1957 as one of the first industrial
engineering consultancy companies to appear on the
Spanish market.

In Spain, the engineering industry began to develop
between 1955 and 1960, and it increased in size in parallel
with the country's economic growth up until 1970. In
common with the whole economy in Spain, the engineering sector was adversely affected by the recession between
1976 and 1980, and during this time there was a 5%
reduction in the number of people employed in the industry.
The larger companies were even more severely affected,
suffering, sometimes, a 25% reduction in their workforces.

A Spanish Association of Engineering Consultants
(ASINCE) was formed in 1975 and a Spanish Association
of Consulting and Engineering Companies (ASEINCO)
in 1977. In 1986 70% of the people in the engineering
industry were employed by the group of companies
forming ASEINCO.

Four stages can be distinguished in the development of IDOM:

- an initial stage of slow, steady growth between 1957 and 1965 when the company employed 129 people

- a developmental stage from 1970 until 1976 when the company diversified and grew to employ 220 people

- a crisis period of zero growth from 1976 until 1981, during which no profits were made and the number of employees remained static

- a consolidation stage from 1981 until 1986 during which the company achieved a significant increase in its business activities, increasing its staff to 295, of whom 136 are university graduates.

In 1986 IDOM was among the top ten Spanish engineering companies. It operates in most sectors of the economy in Spain, and has assignments in seven South American countries and in Africa.

Currently IDOM works mainly for medium-sized companies, helping them to develop corporate strategy, to improve materials management (for manufacturing companies), and to analyse and improve their organization structures. IDOM is also concerned with assisting governmental bodies in the analysis of industrial structures and the development of policies to assist smaller and medium-sized companies.

2   Policy/philosophy

The founder and first President of the company laid down some principles on which the company should be run. These principles have been used consistently; particular emphasis has been given to the following statement about the company:

An association of professionals of which the main aim is human development and increased technical competence. Giving opportunities to all of them, promoting them, assuming higher risks – when assigning them responsibilities – than what is considered common by other engineering companies, and keeping capital ownership only and exclusively for those who work in IDOM.

During the stressful period 1975 to 1980 the company decided to introduce, with the help of a group of external consultants, the concept of Strategic Management. The aim was to interpret the above statement of principle in the light of the prevailing situation: to develop the human potential of the company to meet the needs of the evolving market place.

A scan of the market place made it clear that IDOM's customers needed not just an engineering service, but a service where the economic aspects were fully taken into account and business management skills were exercised. The demands of the market place were influenced by political changes in the Spanish State, by changes in the way public administration was conducted, and by the negotiations for entry into the European Economic Community – in addition to the overriding economic problems at that time.

The need to involve key members of the workforce in the formulation of this strategic management plan was evident. In 1978, 12 people played a full part in forming the strategy: in 1981 it was 20 and by 1985 no less than 32 people were closely involved in formulating the company strategy. Involving people was seen as a key to gaining commitment, and helping the workforce to understand and adapt to the changes which were vital to survival, and ultimately, for success and growth.

The first strategic plan, formulated in 1978, highlighted a number of weaknesses which IDOM had to tackle. They were:

- a need for a number of IDOM engineers to improve their knowledge in areas such as energy, concrete, electronics, natural gas and related construction work

- a need for an international perspective, and for IDOM engineers to travel abroad to understand changes in the market place and the developing technologies

– a need for senior engineers to be more competent commercially and in negotiating and securing contracts

– a need for the training of technical managers to include business management.

At the same time, it was recognized that IDOM's strength was in its independent association of professional people, coupled with its reputation for quality of service to the customer. Any changes introduced had to safeguard these two essential features of success.

In order to broaden the base of its operation IDOM decided to accept assignments in consortia with well known foreign companies, with the condition that the foreign companies help to train IDOM's staff in new areas of expertise. Where appropriate, IDOM also made temporary contracts with leading consultants, collaborating with them on key assignments over extended periods of time.

To further develop a more competent workforce, IDOM also decided to create interdisciplinary teams and to recruit holders of masters' degrees (MBAs) who had previously studied engineering.

3   Continuous development practice

Some of the key procedures adopted by IDOM in following through its desire to maintain and to upgrade the competence of its professional workforce include:

(a)   Strategic review meetings, which are held each year in October and are attended by all the senior engineers and most of the junior engineers. The aim of each of these meetings is to involve key people in discussions which will enable them to understand more fully the company's strategic objectives, the strategic management models used, the current information about the company and its position.

(b) Contracts with consultants of high standing (12 so far) who bring new ideas and thinking to the company as they help IDOM's staff to grapple with difficult contracts and as they direct teams formed from IDOM's engineering specialists.

(c) Technical seminars, usually one day in length, where a specialist within IDOM explains a subject of interest and concern to other members of staff: originally, technical subjects were dealt with, but now commercial subjects are covered, and matters such as relations with customers, human relations problems, team-working, assignment management and economic analysis. In most of these seminars case studies were used which had been written by company staff, based on actual situations within IDOM. Four of these case studies are now used regularly in the Masters' programme (MBA) at the Institute of Higher Business Studies (IESE), which is part of Spain's University of Navarra. The case studies are introduced by members of the Board of Directors of IDOM.

(d) Attendance, by six people between 1980 and 1985, at the Advanced Management Programme at IESE.

(e) Participation by ten of IDOM's senior executives in several Associations, Institutions, Discussion Groups, and Seminars has been encouraged and facilitated; in a few special cases executives have joined the boards of directors of some business companies.

(f) Recruitment of MBA graduates (one in 1982, three in 1983, two in 1984, and three in 1985) from the IESE Masters' programme. These graduates have been integrated into the company.

(g) A series of meetings (25 in all lasting from two to four hours each) were held to help newly recruited engineers and MBA graduates to understand the

company, its history, its approach towards work
and its attitude towards customers. These meetings were not compulsory and about half of those
invited actually attended the sessions.

(h) A series of half-day, informal seminars on the last
Saturday each month where well known national
experts lead discussions on topical subjects such
as Spanish integration into the EC, human
organizations and motivation.

4   Problems

One problem arose from the need to move the company
into Strategic Management. The first challenge was to
convince senior engineers that this was the right direction
in which to move.

Considerable effort has been directed towards helping
senior engineers to prepare themselves and their subordinates to undertake consultancy work in the field of
Strategic Management.

A further problem has been the reluctance of some
consultants to take an international perspective and to be
prepared to travel abroad to undertake assignments. This
has been a particular problem for people living in the
Basque region.

As the company has grown in size, it has become more
difficult to be open with all members of staff about the
longer term plans of the organization.

5   Results and achievements

The efforts described above, which arose out of the
strategic planning exercises of the late '70s and of the early
'80s, resulted in an expansion of the company and highly
profitable performance in 1984, 1985 and 1986.

In 1986, the company realized a turnover of 1,400
million Pesetas, and a profit of 140 million Pesetas, with
306 employees. Over the year the company undertook
250 contracts.

The company is determined to use a proportion of these profits to further develop the competence of its people and hence secure the future prosperity of the company. IDOM has now turned its attention to two key challenges:

(a) to define the services and quality levels which will be required for the 1990s, and

(b) to decide where the effort in terms of people development should now be directed.

6 Oxfordshire District Health Authority
Continuous development within a health authority

1 Background data

This case history records three independent examples of the introduction of continuous development (CD) practice in a large organization employing some 10,000 people in eight Units.

Recently the management of the Health Authority has been changed so that there is a District General Manager supported by an Executive Board which includes two Assistant General Managers, one responsible for planning and performance and the other for personnel and administration. Each Unit has a General Manager in charge, who is responsible for day to day operations. These managers have a great deal of autonomy within the general guidelines and budgets laid down by the Authority.

Responsibility for training is shared between:

A Training & Development Officer, based in the head-quarters of the District Health Authority, who reports to an Assistant District General Manager (Personnel & Administration). This person reports to the District General Manager.

The Unit Personnel Officers who have a training budget allocated from the Centre. Some management training is organized and paid for by the District.

A centrally based Nursing Training Officer who administers a training budget allocated to Senior Nursing Officers in the Units, for statutory training. Other training, including management training, is organized from the Centre. The training given is mainly concerned with clinical updating.

In 1985 all the senior managers attended a two-day workshop at which a draft Training and Development Strategy was drawn up. This strategy is intended to improve the managerial commitment to training and to introduce performance appraisal on a wider scale. The strategy is concerned mainly with training, rather than with CD.

2   Policy/philosophy

The District Training Officer is attempting to persuade managers to take a more personal and direct interest in the training of their staff. Traditionally, managers have nominated people for courses organized by the Centre or by the Personnel Officers in the Units. Two main factors are causing managers to query the effectiveness of this approach. The first is the general impetus from the National Health Service Training Authority (NHSTA) to ensure that training is more directly related to work. The second is that, in a situation where money is tight, sending staff on courses haphazardly is not the best use of the available funds. The District Training Officer is attempting to persuade managers to recognize that the concepts of CD offer a means for using scarce training funds in an effective way. Although the term CD is not used, the phrase 'training & development' is used to imply the same thing, particularly to engender the idea that sending people on courses is not the sole means of fostering learning.

This idea is also being promoted by NHSTA who are encouraging Districts to make temporary transfers of potential high fliers, at various levels, to 'learning posts'. This can be used by the District Training Officer as a means of encouraging managers to take a greater personal interest in the training of their own staff. One example of this is a radiographer who applied unsuccessfully for a post in the planning department. The individual's potential was recognized, and she is now spending a year seconded to planning as a means of encouraging her general development.

However, it must be said that these are isolated instances. Although the District Training Officer, encouraged by the District General Manager, has a clear idea of what should be achieved, the introduction of a generally recognized and accepted CD philosophy is still in its early stages. Section 3.2 below, relating to nursing staff on one ward, may however prove to be of particular significance in that it demonstrates the benefits of CD in practice.

3 Continuous development practice

The first part of this section is concerned with the attempt of the District Training Officer to introduce the concepts of CD into the development of staff in the Units. The second part illustrates how CD has arisen as a result of a change in policy related to the professional staffing of one ward in one Unit. This change involved giving the nursing staff responsibility for making certain decisions relating to patient care which had previously been made by doctors. The third outlines the efforts of a specialist department to improve its efficiency through the application of CD principles.

3.1 *CD for managers*

A starting point some years ago was to run a series of courses for managers in conjunction with Oxford Polytechnic. These courses were novel to the Authority in two major respects:

(1) the participants came from a variety of disciplines

(2) they included project work.

The courses have now been refined so that there is a basic one-week management course, followed by a series of two or three-day modules which can be taken on an 'à la carte' basis. These modules include, for example, communications, interviewing and employee relations. There is also on offer a module concerned with Resource Management which is based on a work project. Senior management involvement in the results of this training is patchy, but there are indications that the Resource Management projects have resulted in senior managers taking a considerable interest in the projects undertaken by their subordinates. Additionally the District Training Officer has been involved in a review of the courses with the senior managers and their subordinates some three months after they have taken place. There is no doubt that these reviews have acted as a spur to senior managers to take a greater personal interest in the development of their subordinates. Building on this foundation, the District Training Officer intends to develop further actions which will encourage and enable managers to take a greater personal continuing interest in their subordinates' development.

3.2   *CD in nursing*

One of the more remarkable instances of the development of CD resulting from a major change in working practice has occurred in relation to an experiment concerning nursing practice. In 1974 a new Chief Nursing Officer developed a philosophy that nursing, in its own right, provided a therapy for patients. In a limited number of areas in the Authority it is now the policy that each patient should have a named nurse, and that each nurse should be individually responsible and accountable for named patients. Thus:

– the individual nurse is responsible and accountable for her own decisions and actions

– she must be able to defend those decisions and actions as being in the best interests of her patients

> – she must only undertake work for which she is trained and which she is competent to perform.

We examined this philosophy in one ward in the Radcliffe Hospital in Oxford.

This ward deals with four types of patient:

- orthopaedic
- amputations after-care
- strokes
- hysterectomies.

The philosophy demanded a number of significant changes:

(1) A contraction in the chain of command. Nurses report directly to the Ward Sister who reports directly to the Director of Nursing Services.

(2) Auxiliary nurses and orderlies have been dispensed with.

(3) The Ward Sister has her own budget.

(4) Ward sisters are helped by 'nursing practitioners' who provide expertise and coaching.

(5) The ward has a named doctor who is part of the team and helps nurses to expand their expertise, and carries out examinations of patients.

(6) Physiotherapists, social workers and occupational therapists are used as 'consultants' to the team.

The learning process for nurses has been revolutionized. Only a limited use is made of courses. Most learning takes place through:

- coaching by the Ward Sister and the nursing practitioners

- ward seminars are held, in the nurses' own time, to discuss problems. This is 'not a problem because the nurses are interested'

- peer discussion and learning.

A 'care plan' is developed for each patient, the patient taking part in its discussion and compilation. In this way the nurse and the Ward Sister become key people in patient care, and also in the management structure.

Results

Some assessment of the results has been carried out against a control group:

- discharged patients were more independent and could do more for themselves

- patients expressed more satisfaction with the care they had received in hospital

- six months after discharge, patients were more satisfied with their quality of life

- patients spent less time in an NHS bed than the control group.

There is thus some evidence that because of this last factor, and the lack of auxiliaries and orderlies, costs have been reduced. (Nursing staff costs account for a major part of hospital budgets.)

Comments of a nurse

Nurse Easterbrook has been on this ward for 2 months. Her comments are instructive:

I have had to learn a great deal. For example about massage, reflex actions in the foot, and about strokes.

I work with a nurse practitioner who is more experienced in this type of nursing. He isn't my boss, but he helps me to learn what I need to learn. I ask him questions. Most learning takes place on the ward. He will arrange for specialists to come on the ward – or I may attend a lecture which he arranges for me.

I've never been encouraged to learn in this way before.

The job is less frustrating. In previous jobs I used to feel tired and jobs were left undone. Now I have time to care for patients. You're responsible for patients. You get involved with their families, give them counselling and listen to their comments. Sister used to do that sort of thing – now they are my patients.

When someone goes away on a course, or has read something, they tell us about it at a ward seminar, which we attend in our own time.

To work this system you need people who are sympathetic to the ideas – it's a different culture.

3.3 CD in the chiropody department

The manager's view

The chiropody department has 19 full-time staff, supplemented by sessional staff. It provides a service throughout the Health Authority. Until recently the waiting lists were considered excessive. In the words of Mr Joyce, the District Chiropodist:

In our department we've moved towards agreeing operational goals. We had to ask if we delivered our skills in the best way, given the shortage of resources.

This is another example of CD being stimulated by changes in the way work is performed.

Mr Joyce felt that CD and the courses mentioned on page 91 were linked. The training budget for the chiropody department works out at £25 per head per year. To quote Mr Joyce again:

Limited resources have forced me to look at means of learning other than courses.

CD in chiropody is based round staff meetings and appraisal. Staff meetings are held every two months and are used to discuss both professional and managerial information. Members of the department who have attended courses are expected to report on what they have learned and this is used as a basis for group discussion and learning. Mr Joyce again:

You need to supplement in-house training with outside courses in order to gain knowledge.

The effect of this is that a group member attends outside courses not solely for his/her own benefit, but for the benefit of the group.

Mr Joyce introduced a self-appraisal system, with the aim of encouraging people to think about what they were doing, how they were doing it and to tease out their ideas for improvement. He feels:

The biggest block is lack of information. When people are given information then people become involved.

CD is a frame of mind. The more stimulating the work, the more people want to learn. There is more professional discussion among individuals, so that CD feeds on itself.

I see my role as a leader of the group trying to get results happening.

We need to create an environment where people are stimulated to keep up-to-date. It is the work which provides the stimulation.

The result of these changes has been a 75% reduction of waiting lists.

A Senior Chiropodist's view

The views of Mr L King, a Senior Chiropodist in the department, complemented his manager's statements. Mr King offered an incisive comment about training in the NHS:

Managers tend to come up through the ranks and are given little management training. They are checked in and move from crisis to crisis. Courses tend to teach the buzz words like 'objectives' and 'results'. More structured training related to a philosophy is required. It is easier to send someone on a course than to make time for coaching, particularly when there are staff shortages.

Mr King felt that the appraisal process had been successful in promoting new ideas. He also felt that the 'effective presentation' module he had attended had given him the confidence to present his ideas.

Overall Mr King felt that:

> If CD is going to happen, senior management need to make it clear that people are their greatest resource. They can do this by involving them in decision making. This is beginning to happen in chiropody.

He also had a salutary warning:

> If nothing gets done in terms of job enrichment, people will leave.

4 Problems

In the District Training Officer's view the major hurdle to be surmounted is to get people to recognize the link between personal and organizational development. This involves developing with managers objectives for each department, and the associated learning needs required to achieve the objectives. There is no appraisal system in operation below general manager level, but this is being encouraged by the NHSTA and will be developed to include other staff during the next few years. The District Training Officer intends that any appraisal system will *not* be linked to pay. The problem of gaining direct manager involvement in the development of their subordinates is the key to the introduction of a CD philosophy. The District Training Officer intends to hold meetings and discussions about the philosophy, and to offer information about what can be achieved. The case example of the nursing staff may prove helpful in this.

5 Results and achievements

This case example has outlined two distinct approaches to the introduction of CD – first, a general move throughout the District which is still in the embryonic stage, and secondly, much more rapid advances in one ward and one department, where a revolutionary approach to work organization necessitated the practice of CD if the experiments were to succeed.

In neither instance was the term CD used, nor were the principles set out in the IPM Code 'Continuous Development: People and Work' consciously applied. In the first example, a desire to use scarce training resources more effectively provided the incentive; in the case of the ward and the chiropody department, CD arose because it was the only practical means of achieving the results needed. There may be a general lesson here – namely that CD will be most easily introduced where a revolution in the organization of work takes place. (See also the Babcock Power case example.)

Where a more general approach to the introduction of CD takes place the major hurdle is the attitude of managers. A major achievement in this case example has been to help managers in general to recognize that there is an essential difference between traditional knowledge training and the learning required to apply that knowledge effectively.

7 Toshiba Consumer Products (UK) Limited
Continuous development within a Japanese controlled company in the UK

1 Background data

This case history is of interest because, although the company does not use the term continuous development (CD), through the introduction of a Japanese management philosophy most of the 'Results' in the IPM's Code 'Continuous Development: People and Work' have become discernible. As in some other case examples, the trigger for this state of affairs has been a profound change in the organization of work rather than a conscious attempt to introduce a CD philosophy.

Toshiba agreed to dissolve its partnership with the Rank Organization in 1981. The result was an immediate reduction in the workforce to some 300 people, with some 2,500 people being made redundant. The company makes TV, video products and microwave ovens.

The new company has been successful and the workforce has grown steadily so that today nearly 1,000 are employed. Turnover has risen from £14m to £100m in 5 years. This growth has created opportunities for promotion and the company has encouraged employees to learn and to grow with their jobs.

2   Policy/philosophy

Toshiba's corporate philosophy includes the aim to utilize resources effectively and 'provide. . .staff members with the opportunity to realize their full potential and cultivate their abilities to the utmost'. From the start, Toshiba created an egalitarian plant. This involved, for example, the creation of open plan offices (the Managing Director has a desk in the open office), everyone uses the same canteen (Toshiba call it a restaurant), and all employees, including the Managing Director, wear a standard uniform. This has led to the breaking down of traditional attitudes both to work, to the way objectives are achieved and to the relationship between management and workers, as well as between different working groups. One observer has written:

> By definition, you can't be an effective Toshiba manager without feeling that all men really are equal, and that the idea of 'the team' is an eternal truth.
>
> (Ivor Williams, 'Toshiba's British Switch', *Management Today*, March 1984.)

3   Continuous development practice

3.1   *Basic planks*

Seven planks were identified by which this basic philosophy is translated into practice. They are presented in no particular order because the company believes that it is the totality of the approach, rather than any individual item of practice, which matters.

(1) People are expected to work to a manual of procedures (a training manual). All training is done on-the-job with supervisors responsible for ensuring that new starters are correctly trained. There is also a short period of induction off-the-job.

(2) Once these procedures have been mastered, workers are allowed scope to develop new hand movements. Any other changes from procedure laid down in the manual have to be authorized. This is done by the worker talking to his/her superior. The worker must receive an evaluated response stating whether the idea can be accepted, and if not why not.

(3) The procedures demand a very high standard of output, quality and waste control. There is great attention to detail.

(4) There has been some experimentation with small group activity (Quality Circles). These have proved successful and it is intended to develop them on a wider basis.

(5) There are regular visits of teams of auditors from Japan (financial, manufacturing and systems specialists) who draw attention to any lowering of standards.

(6) The Managing Director spends time visiting all areas of the company and encouraging staff to talk to him about problems, difficulties and successes. He is a good listener.

(7) There is a stated policy of preferring internal candidates for promotion.

3.2   *Organization*

Managers are expected to be their own personnel managers. The personnel department consists of a Personnel Director, a Personnel Officer and their secretaries. The role of this team is to offer general advice – not to take decisions for managers.

3.3   *Personnel practices*

There are no job descriptions. To quote the Personnel Director:

> Everyone is free to expand his/her job to the limit of his/her capability.

This manifests itself at the workforce level in the grading system. There is no job evaluation, each new employee being placed on grade 1. Within the first year he/she is encouraged to master three of 17 skills (for example, soldering, mechanical assembly, inspection). When the three chosen skills are mastered the individual is promoted to grade 2. Every area of the factory, including the office, is covered by this system.

The next step is to become a 'sub-key' operator. In effect this is someone who can stand in for absentees and be responsible for the standard of output and quality of a group of between 8 and 15 people.

'Sub-key' operators can aspire to becoming 'key operators' who stand in for supervisors and are capable of line preparation, training and similar tasks. In effect they are assistant supervisors in that they are also responsible for the work of a number of sub-key operators. Supervisors are likely to be chosen from the ranks of 'key' operators.

The important thing about this progression is that people are offered the incentive and opportunity to grow on the job if they wish to make the effort. Taken together with the regular team meetings and the general philosophy of Toshiba we have the crucial elements of CD.

3.4   *Meetings*

To quote the Personnel Director again:

> The whole place is based on daily and weekly meetings which bring problems to light.

Individual and group coaching is a way of life rather than a stereotyped technique. There is an annual appraisal system which concentrates on people's development.

Additionally, there are monthly and bi-annual meetings at which the company's performance and progress are discussed.

4   **Problems**

Three main problems and one potential problem have been identified. The problems were:

(a)   Creating a new attitude to work and factory relationships within the workforce. This was tackled by careful selection. In the Managing Director's words:

> We were more interested in people with the right attitudes rather than with high levels of expertise, as we can teach them how to perform their role, but to change bad attitudes is difficult if not impossible.

The creation of positive attitudes is also helped by the fact that there are few levels of management, which makes communication much easier.

(b)   Difficulties in introducing a simple, uniform, factory-wide grading scheme. For example, the storemen thought that they were worth more than operators.

(c)   In the early days there was a high turnover of supervisors. Many found that they were unable to perform in their new role as real leaders of a team of people.

The potential problem is what will happen when growth levels out? It is possible that people's willingness to learn and to develop is linked to the opportunities for promotion which have arisen from the company's rapid growth.

5 Results and achievements

The major result is, of course, the growth of the company. In terms of CD the observer must be impressed by every employee's desire to learn, to grow on the job and to contribute to the well-being of the whole. To quote the Managing Director again:

> We have no individual job descriptions because we all have the same task – to contribute to the profitability of the company.

Assessment by a Manager

Mr Bill Lockwood is a Production Manager who has worked on the site for 17 years. He commented:

> Relationships have totally changed: the management style is different. Previously it was 'them' and 'us' with little communication between management and the shop floor. People were told when management had decided something. Now they are involved via meetings or the Company Advisory Board before a final decision is made so that they can make suggestions and have an input. It also gives them time to adjust to the new idea. When a new system is developed, Toshiba development engineers work closely with people on the shop floor. Previously many new ideas failed because there was little shop floor input.

Commenting on Toshiba's approach in general, Mr Lockwood made four incisive comments:

> I couldn't be a manager here unless I was prepared to accept the team approach, which in my eyes means that I am only as good as the people who work for me. If I

don't train them correctly, give them the right information and guide them, they won't perform to my standards.
I will only reap what I sow.

My experience of British management is that when
faced with a problem they will either take the short
option or try and bulldoze their own solution through
with little consultation with the people it will affect. In
many cases it could be that they are stifled by strong
union intervention and are forced into these situations
which result in a wrong decision for all concerned,
employees, union and management. Here, we discuss
openly with the union and members the causes of the
problem and what solutions we can reach to overcome
it, for the benefit of all.

I would like to feel that people will still want to
develop even if the company stops growing. Even if we
stop growing there will always be challenges to keep
people motivated.

What Toshiba does is only common sense – it's treating people with respect and valuing their contribution.

Assessment by a Senior Supervisor

Mrs Val Cann is a Senior Supervisor. She has spent 32
years on the site.

Mrs Cann liked working for Rank, but she has noticed
some major differences:

The communications are better here and you're more
involved with management. You're part of the family
and are free to speak your mind. We encourage people
to talk and not to feel that what they say will be held
against them.

Of course we need rules – but they are to keep order
in the family.

During the induction training, we encourage people
to talk to us – to tell us what they think and what they'd
change.

We are encouraged to learn and we're given coaching by our managers. We're encouraged to think for
ourselves.

> If I go away on a course I'm going for the whole of my group, not just for myself. For example, when I went to Japan we all discussed what I'd seen and learned.

Assessment by a sub-key operator

Mrs Wendy Bennett has been on the site for 5½ years. She came from Liverpool and expected that working on the site would be 'just another job'. She is surprised that she has 'got so far'. She was encouraged to apply for promotion and remarks on her increase in self confidence:

> I've been encouraged to take more responsibility. They try to get you to grow.
>
> You are kept informed. I'm not saying that I understand all the financial information, but you get a general idea.
>
> In my last job I was in the union and they gave you all the information. Here I'm not in a union but I get as much information as if I was in one.
>
> I'm encouraged to learn. I'm guided by several supervisors. That's interesting because you get different approaches and then can make up your own mind.

The last word must lie with Mr Des Thomson, the Managing Director:

> Continuous development must stem spontaneously from basic management attitudes to the way it respects and treats people. It must not be allowed to become a 'system' like Management by Objectives.

8 Babcock Energy Limited
Continuous development within a heavy engineering company

1 Background data

The Power Division of Babcock Energy Limited designs and constructs defence equipment and steam generating plant for power stations. This case example is concerned with the design department based in London. This unit is part of the responsibility of a Technical Director. There is also a Management Services Director for Systems and Computing responsible for providing a computer based service to the design department. In simplified form the basic structure is as follows:

Board Director ——————— Board Director
| |
Research and Design   Computer and
| Management Services
Professional Engineers |
and Draughtsmen   Technical Systems Analysts

Organizationally, the cross-over point between the two functions is at Board level. Traditionally, Management Services provided a service for Research and Design concerned with making the old computer software work. This case example will indicate how the staff of the Management Services Department (MSD) became much more closely integrated with members of the Research and Design Department.

The spur for this change was the introduction of Computer-Graphics, Augmented Design and Manufacture (CADAM). The company was interested in finding ways of making CADAM work, rather than in introducing continuous development. Essentially, CADAM is a design tool able to investigate the effects of changes in design which can influence the work of designers. Before the introduction of CADAM, new designs were developed by professional engineers who called on MSD for a service which was concerned mainly with basic calculations rather than with fundamental changes in design, that is, answering 'what if ...?' type of questions.

One result of CADAM has been to form teams where draughtsmen take more responsibility for basic design (that is, do some of the work previously done by professional engineers), allowing the professional engineers more time to concentrate on fundamental product development. For this to work MSD staff needed to be integrated as a part of the total design team. The design function is now organized so that there are relatively small teams composed of professional engineers, draughtsmen and MSD staff.

2 Policy/philosophy

The company believes that the starting point for staff development is the identification of learning needs and the evolution of practices which will meet those needs. The use of CD practices during the introduction of CADAM illustrates the point. As learning needs became apparent, managers, employees and the Training Officer thought through how they would best be met.

In the future, this pattern will be continued and it is now the company's intention to develop a full continuous development policy. Until then, it will consider each new situation on its merits and take the steps which it considers appropriate to meet the day to day learning needs which arise.

3 The introduction of CADAM
(Continuous development practice)

In order to understand how the present design teams operate and how a philosophy of CD has evolved, it is necessary to relate how CADAM was introduced.

In 1983 a grant of £112,000 was made to the company from the EC Social Fund for training related to CADAM and other new technology. This grant was made to help a traditional engineering company adapt and to train its staff in order to compete worldwide. All the training took place in-house.

There were three phases of training:

- learning to use the equipment (knowledge training). This was done on four-week courses run by company trainers who were themselves trained by IBM (the suppliers of CADAM equipment)

- guided experience of the equipment

- continuous development.

The company trainers were Senior Draughtsmen. They held senior positions in the old drawing office and were interested in CADAM and its development. Mr John Willis, the Training Officer, stated that 'the trainers selected themselves' in the sense that, of the people considered for the role, only a proportion indicated sufficient natural interest and flair. These trainers also assumed a development design role in that they also played a part in developing the software for CADAM.

This is significant because instead of using 'training staff' who were responsible only for 'training', the trainers themselves were deeply involved in the development of CADAM and were not directly responsible to the training department. This has important implications for CD because it implies that the people responsible for 'training' are also responsible for part of the work for which people are being trained. In this sense the word 'training' is inappropriate. A better description is that certain staff were selected to help others to learn what they themselves had learnt and were continuing to learn. The role of the 'trainer' was, therefore, to ensure that everyone affected by CADAM was kept up to date and fully informed. (Phases 2 and 3 of the training.)

We turn now to the role of the Management Services Department which provides the back-up service for CADAM. Members of MSD were involved with IBM in the original training. Today they assume an important role within the Engineering Design Department. It will be remembered that originally MSD staff were solely concerned with ensuring that the software functioned properly. Now the professional engineers originate changes in the computer software themselves but call on MSD staff for help and advice with problems.

The result of all these changes is that there is a much closer liaison between the professional engineers, draughtsmen and MSD, with the roles of each merging and overlapping. MSD staff are located in the next office to the CADAM development office. They work as teams on a project as opposed to each group having clearly defined responsibilities which can be written down on a job description.

Each team has a designated professional engineer as team leader. Originally, of course, there had always been team meetings, but the form of these meetings has changed dramatically. In the pre CADAM days each member reported 'to the boss' in turn so that the meeting tended to be a series of individual reports. Today every member of the team is encouraged to make a contribution on any topic under discussion. This, of course, has led to considerable overlap of responsibilities, so that the members of the team work as a group rather than as individuals. The result has been a much improved capacity to solve problems.

A further important development has been that the chairman of the meeting is not always the most senior member of the team. Instead, the individual responsible for a particular aspect, whatever his status, takes the chair during discussion of his special concerns.

4   Appraisal and training

The need now is to develop a common understanding of what each individual's role is about. This work is in progress but in the words of Mr Stuart Bannister, the Management Development Manager:

> Things are developing so fast that it is like attempting to shoot at a moving target.

Part of the answer is thought to be in preparing role and grade descriptions, and there have been instances of people moving through grades because of their increased contribution to the work of a team.

The annual appraisal interview is taking a new form. There is increased concentration on discussion of problems related to the whole job and the working of the teams, as opposed to a more formal and stilted discussion about each item on the old job descriptions. This, in turn, has led to a more dynamic discussion of the individual's learning/coaching needs both in respect of his technical abilities and of his contribution as a team member.

The Training Officer has now prepared a menu of short courses to meet these needs. They include courses on public speaking, holding meetings and report writing.

A design draughtsman was appointed as Training Officer. Previously each section (MSD, draughtsmen, professional engineers) had its own training expertise and arrangements. Today the training function has a co-ordinating role in making learning facilities, knowledge and experience available to anyone across the company. For example, if a draughtsman wishes to learn about a particular topic he contacts the training department which, if it is agreed with his manager, will put him in contact with the appropriate person, either inside or outside the company. The training department has thus assumed a learning information function – a facilitating role.

An important role of the training department is to ensure that individuals talk to their managers about their learning requirements. The company handbook states that 'managers are responsible for the training of their staff'. In order to make this requirement come alive, the Training Officer helps individuals to formulate the relevant topics on which they should seek advice and coaching from their managers. If the individual finds difficulty in communicating with his manager, the Training Officer will assist by discussing with the manager how he can help.

5   Problems

No major problems arose in relation to CD. A way was found for satisfying each need as it arose.

One interesting example was the perceived need to ensure that the knowledge and experience gained by one team was transferred and made available to other teams. A Computer Policy Committee, made up of members of senior management, advised by a sub-committee of staff from both Engineering and MSD, discharges this responsibility.

6   Results and achievements

6.1   *Views of senior management*

Mr John Varney, the CADAM co-ordinator (the senior manager in charge of its introduction), made a number of important points about the introduction of CD:

- It is essential to set up teams of people who talk together.

- It is essential to encourage people to come to me to make suggestions as opposed to waiting for me to tell them what to do next.

- We need continually to update our courses for new entrants in order to ensure that they are acquainted with our latest thinking.

Mr Varney was asked whether, on reflection, he had learned anything about the introduction of CD which could be applied if he had to start again in another context. He identified eight key stages:

(1) First he would identify the structures and networks which existed for producing the required work outputs.

(2) He would then identify the essential interfaces between the various networks.

(3) During his discussions with staff he would encourage them to think about their role in the total work output systems.

(4) Next he would bring together the senior people in charge of each network for them to discuss how well the networks meshed together, and to identify problems in this process of 'meshing'.

(5) The next step would be to bring together people at a more junior level from each network, where their work impacted on another network, in order to highlight problem areas.

(6) Armed with case examples from 3, 4 and 5 above, he would then help supervisors to appreciate that their major role was to control the outputs of work, as opposed to attempting to control every detail of input. This is essential if people are to be encouraged to think about how to overcome problems.

(7) When some momentum had been gained, he would encourage teams to review the benefits of the new ways of working. Mr Varney clearly recognized the importance of building on success.

(8) Finally Mr Varney stressed that, once started, the process of encouraging people to talk to people must continue. 'We can't stop because we are being driven by new developments which are the result of our teams.'

A moment's reflection will show that these eight points are applicable in any situation – not just the introduction of CADAM. Notably, computer aided design has been introduced in other factories without the benefits of CD and team working. In those situations the introduction of CADAM has resulted only in being an aid to the draughtsman's traditional job, without enhancingg his responsibilities and releasing his inheeent talents.

6.2   *Views of a draughtsman*

The reactions of a draughtsman, who had worked in the drawing office before and during the introduction of CADAM, are also of interest. His first overall reactions were:

I get more job satisfaction – it is no longer a run of the mill job. I make more inputs into designs.

During the discussion he made the following observations which indicate how well CD had taken root:

- When I learn it may be by trial and error, or I may go to someone else and ask for help.

- The present arrangements encourage people to ask 'why couldn't we do it this way?'

- There has been a change in management style. In the old days we were not encouraged to challenge the established way of doing things.

- I can now put my own thoughts into CADAM. Before, we worked mechanically.

- I can go into anyone else's file. I've got access to much more information than before.

His final summary was, perhaps, crucial:

Nothing must go wrong with the team-work, otherwise we would be thoroughly demoralized. Previously a draughtsman's work was individual and bore his hallmark. Today everything is the result of team effort. This requires a new way of thinking.

A major conclusion from this case is that the need for CD has stemmed from day to day operational needs arising from CADAM, not from a deliberate act of corporate policy. (Interestingly, the points made under the 'Results' section of the IPM's Code 'Continuous Development: People and Work' are all present.)

The company's experience indicates that as the practice of CD evolves, traditional approaches to writing job descriptions and the appraisal process are likely to require modification.

Finally, the role of the 'trainer' changes profoundly. Instead of being a course arranger and provider, he becomes a catalyst for learning, working closely on a day to day basis with operational teams. His professional learning expertise assists line managers to sharpen their perception of the learning needs of their teams.

9   Bank of England
Continuous development within the financial sector

1   Background data

The Bank of England is Britain's central bank. Set up in 1694 as a company to lend capital to Government, the growth of its role and significance is a central part of the nation's economic history. By 1766 it had become the government banker and acted as manager and registrar of government securities. It was nationalized in 1946 (and was given a new Royal Charter) and so it was no longer owned by private shareholders as it had been for over two hundred and fifty years.

The Bank is now a department of Government but works closely with the Treasury, the Foreign and Commonwealth Office and the Department of Trade and Industry. It advises the Government on financial policy development and is responsible for implementing such government policies. As it operates, it is in effect the Government's major link with the financial community.

It has close relationships with international and financial markets and institutions such as the International Monetary Fund, the World Bank and OECD, thereby having a considerable influence on worldwide financial affairs.

Domestically, it is responsible for issuing banknotes, about seven and a half million of which are printed daily; a similar number of old notes are destroyed. Indeed the printing works is the largest department within the Bank.

Less visible, to the general public at least, but more important, are its technical banking activities which have several facets:

Banking: The Bank of England holds the main banking accounts of the Government. As a result, eventually all tax revenue is received by the Bank and all government payments originate from it.

It also holds accounts of the major 'high street' banks, who keep substantial deposits from which to settle each day the cheques and credit transfers which they have handled amongst themselves.

Many overseas banks also have a accounts with the Bank of England.

Government Borrowing: The Bank raises finance for the Public Sector Borrowing Requirement by borrowing in London's financial markets. It issues new stocks directly to the public or sells them on the Stock Exchange in the 'gilt-edged' market.

It keeps records of stockholders, makes the appropriate interest payments and makes the repayments when they are due.

Besides this longer term borrowing, the bank raises short-term money by issuing three-monthly Treasury Bills.

Managing the Money Market: The Bank has the responsibility for ensuring the banking system has sufficient cash to meet its day to day requirements. It does this mainly by buying and selling commercial bills. It is also responsible for the implementation of monetary policy, a large part of which involves controlling short-term interest rates.

The official reserves of gold and foreign exchange are managed by the Bank which intervenes as necessary to influence the external value of sterling.

Supervision: One of the key responsibilities of the Bank is for the orderly and ethical conduct of the financial markets. It has a statutory obligation to ensure that the affairs of banks and deposit takers are conducted properly, largely to protect the interests of the depositors.

This last role illustrates the complexity and fast-changing nature of the environment in which the Bank and its staff operate. Although steeped in history and with many long-established and well-proven practices and conventions, nevertheless the business (for it is a business making an operating profit of nearly £88 million in 1985/86), needs all the creativity, responsiveness and anticipatory qualities often more readily associated with smaller and less mature organizations. The past few years have seen, as the next few years will see, revolutionary changes in products, services and ways of trading in the financial markets at least as great as those in other industries. There have been, and will continue to be, major mergers, acquisitions and radical reformations of organizations conducting business in the markets, just as there have been in other industries. New companies will emerge and some older companies will not survive, at least in their present constitutions. But in the finance sector, in contrast with other industries, there has been and will continue to be for the foreseeable future, a fundamental reshaping of the regulatory systems within which the markets operate. New supervisory bodies are being established, new coalitions formed, new statutory safeguards and new regulatory processes are being introduced.

So the Bank of England's roles within the markets will continue to evolve and its pivotal position will be even more significant.

The challenges anticipated for the future are reflected in the recruitment policies and practices of the present. As the 'Careers for Graduates' recruitment booklet expresses it:

Traditional functions of banker to the banking ssystem, manager of government borrowing, manager of the note issue, regulator of the money supply and government adviser are being extended and re-defined, new ones being acquired and mastered. Within the City of London, changes in the financial markets are introducing complex new questions concerning supervisory responsibility and self-regulation. Changing structures in the securities markets and the developing nature of financial services institutions, pose major problems of control, supervision and management. All these areas provide intellectual, managerial and innovative challenges of the highest order.

As a consequence:

...the Bank needs to recruit people with a combination of ourstanding educational achievements and strong personal qualities. People with the ability to meet and overcome problems, who are able to react quickly to and, where necessary, implement change. People who have the robustness of character to accept responsibility themselves, yet are able to work well as part of a team. Working for the Bank is not easy. It is intellectually stretching and personally demanding. . . .

But these are prospects not only for the graduate entry of whom there were 48 in 1986 out of a total recruitment of 280 or so into banking departments. The same challenges await the 'A' level entrants: 'The work will sometimes test your intellect, sometimes your initiative and even, perhaps, your patience. . .'. So the Bank is seeking people with: '. . .the will to succeed and readiness to work hard to achieve that succcess'. This emphasis on capability and effort is maintained in junior clerical selection where the need also is for 'people who are able to work to very high standards in a large, busy, complex organization'.

2   Policy/philosophy

It is hardly surprising, then that, whatever the entry point, the learning and development is largely through performing the job supported by related off-the-job, and course-based training. Early on, the new recruit can expect a variety of work, with progression determined by achievement and the opportunities which can be realistically made available by the business. Again, whatever the level, whatever the stage in career, advancement is determined primarily on the ability and effort of the member of staff.

But the Bank is not merely 'permissive' in its approach to development and career routing. It is also concerned and actively encouraging. As in many organizations, however, whilst the personnel and training specialists may have a clear vision and professional appreciation of what needs to be done to maintain and develop the people to maintain and develop the business, it is not a simple matter in the Bank to persuade line managers and receive commitment to action, despite support at the highest levels.

The problems are understandable and by no means unique. From the late 1970s, the Bank has been conducting a cost-reduction programme with the commonly experienced restricting impact upon training budget and activity. More significantly, however, with staff numbers declining from some 7,500 to around 5,000, many managers have been confronted with what they perceived to be extremely demanding workloads and insufficient staff to meet all the demands. Not surprisingly, not only was there a reluctance to release people for off-the-job training but some neglect of on-the-job coaching and guidance.

However, the view remained and now is being reaffirmed that the people within the business are its most important asset. This is not just a platitude, because in the case of the Bank the quality of expertise which determines the outcomes and the quality of work done is often very publicly evident and subjected to the most stringent external scrutiny. Errors of judgement, mistakes in information provision and failure to meet operational deadlines could have very damaging repercussions and seriously risk the reputation of the Bank. Traditionally, as in other financial institutions, the need for achievement of the highest standards has led to rather narrow specification of roles, close supervision and direction and through monitoring and checking of performance. Providing for error-free performance can be costly and wasteful of talent, breed an over-cautiousness , a bureaucratizing effect on the way work is done, and stifle innovation even at senior levels.

For some time now it has been appreciated that the Bank's ever-developing role can only be fulfilled by energizing the people, encouraging flexibility and versatility, and that the approach to training and development is a vital means of achieving what is required.

So the approach is as encapsulated in the 1980 statement of training policy:

To further the attainment of the Bank's overall and

local objectives by teaching staff skills, widening their knowledge of the organization and better harnessing their natural talents.

3 Continuous development practice

3.1 *Responsibilities and roles*

The Bank's equivalent of a Board of Directors is its Court. The Governor and Deputy Governor lead a team of four Executive Directors and twelve non-Executive Directors. The non-Executive Directors are drawn from industry, commerce and Trade Unions, and appointed by the Crown on the advice of the Prime Minister. In addition, Associate Directors occupy positions equal to the Executive Directors and attend meetings of Court, although they are not formal members.

The Training Centre reports to the Chief of Corporate Services who reports to an Associate Director (Operations and Services); he in turn is responsible to the Deputy Governor. It is a small area in which a person would spend a two or three years' placement and not usually become a 'permanent' trainer.

The Training Centre provides training on a Bank-wide basis to meet common and shared needs. More specific job-related development needs are a local responsibility. Indeed the Centre is moving from being a training provider to more of an internal consultancy resource. The Centre composes a training manual and a 'handy guide', an abstract of which is distributed to all who have responsibility for supervising the work of other people. The guide forcibly reaffirms the line management responsibility for identifying and meeting the training needs of the staff. However, the reality has been that managers have not found it easy to identify needs, so they are reminded in the guide that:

. . .the starting point when considering training should no longer be the training that is available; rather, managers should be asking themselves whether the job performance of those individuals for whose work they have responsibility could be improved through increased skill, experience or knowledge.

The initiative for taking action. . .now lies firmly with local managers and supervisors.

But the ways in which training and development opportunities are provided share the responsibility quite clearly with the job holder. Graduates for example: '. . . will be expected to make an early and significant contribution' and to do that they have to devote considerable effort to learning and learning fast.

3.2   *Identification of learning opportunities and needs*

Like so many organizations which take training seriously, the Bank uses several approaches to pinpointing what skills, knowledge and competences must be acquired.

For new entrants – junior clerical staff, 'A' level school leavers and graduates – there are generic programmes of induction, guided work experiencce and job progression, and off-the-job courses. The training needs are assumed to be shared in the novices' early days. But it is not a 'sausage factory' or 'jelly mould' approach. For example, junior staff have quarterly performance appraisal discussions in the first year and at least annually subsequently. Strengths and weaknesses are reviewed and plans for the next period are agreed. The plans will have to do with jobs and work projects, training and, not least, performance standards, and targets which are to be achieved in the short term.

Performance appraisal is widely used in the Bank and one of its objectives is the identification of training needs which are recorded and of which the Training Centre is notified. But again, in common with so many other organizations, this process in the Bank has a number of problems associated with it. Efforts are being made to make performance appraisal more achievement orientated, with training explicitly recognized as one means by which objectives can be achieved.

The Training Centre does play its part in determining learning requirements. All the programmes it provides have clearly stated aims and target groups and as part of the process of budgeting and submittting development proposals, the training objectives are scrutinized by senior officials.

3.3 Learner involvement

Apart from the scheduled reviews of performance, learner involvement is encouraged from the earliest career stages. The clerical recruitment pamphlet is unequivocal – 'The jobs you undertake, any promotion you win and responsibility you gain, has to be earned by your own ability. . .'. This integration of competence acquired by doing the work, and achievement determining progression, is reaffirmed strongly throughout the Bank and by the training 'style'. In the management and supervision courses, for example, the emphasis is upon learning by experiencing. The responsibility for self-managing of learning is emphasized by the pre-course briefing meeting between the boss and job-holder to clarify the aims and expected benefits of the training. It is a means of encouraging commitment to active learning which is reinforced by careful post-course debriefing. This builds upon the joint definition and agreement of the needs to be met by the courses before nominations are made.

The reshaping of graduate training also includes stronger encouragement to self-direction, the trainees identifying their own needs and means of satisfying them.

3.4 Learning resources

As the supervisors' training guide states:

The various forms that training can take are almost limitles. They range from enhancing on-the-job knowledge – through further qualification, coaching, background reading and study – to training courses run locally, centrally or externally.

The general approach is to use the learning opportunities which the work itself provides. In early career, the work placement is used to provide operating experience and background knowledge and skill on which future development may be based. A typical emmployee will be expected to have a variety of work tasks before any future specialization. Within the realistic constraints of the business needs, the job-holder progresses to more demanding work. The on-the-job learning is typically supported by 'core' training programmes of personal skills such as writing, presenting, coaching, and technical skills such as bookkeeping and statistics. For supervisors there are managing skills courses and appraisal workshops. Most of these are conducted in-house by the Bank's own staff in the Training Centre or locally, but there are some such as finance and accounting which are conducted by outside consultants. Selected individuals with high potential may be able to attend Business School programmes.

Graduates follow a structured programme of on-the-job guided experience conducted by the line manager, and off-the-job courses overseen by the Training Centre. Many younger employees follow part-time professional qualification courses at colleges or polytechnics for three to four years. This education is encouraged to develop a broad background against which the practical and more specific on-the-job learning takes place.

4   Problems

Moving towards a 'continuous development' approach is not easy. An organization cannot just stop what it is doing, and what may have served it very well in the past, and adopt what sceptics might view as no more than the 'flavour of the month'. Continuous development is more likely to be successfully introduced by adaptation, further improvement in quality of training provision, influencing the influential people in the organization and demonstrating the contribution which developing the people makes to business success. In a professional/technical organization like the Bank there is an advantage in that education and professional competence are generally valued. However, it is often viewed as 'front-loaded': the competence is developed early in career and suffices for the remainder. The people responsible for corporate training in the Bank of England recognize that this is not so. The challenge was, is and will continue to be, to build upon what is established. In doing so they will need to overcome a possible view that 'they are ahead of their time' by managers whose chief priority remains, understandably, getting a lot of work done, on time and to a high standard. Training is well regarded, but sometimes the efforts may be perceived as being too little, too late, partly because of resources, and also, paradoxically, as making too heavy a demand on managers and trainees alike.

The focus on on-the-job learning also brings its problems – there is a danger that the career aspirations of young people particularly, who have had their learning appetites whetted, cannot always be met. Jobs and roles cannot be created artificially and impatience can result from people feeling over-qualified for the work they are given to do.

An added challenge confronting the training/development specialists is to assist the business to move further from increasing productivity through cost-constraint which has been its recent preoccupation, towards productivity achieved through enhanced performance. The Bank is making progress towards this challenge. Although they had a mixed reception by the participants, 'change' workshops led by an external consultant have involved nearly 300 of the most senior staff. There is a general recognition that much more needs to be done to harness the talent of the staff, and the environment for training and development activity is altogether more conducive than it sometimes has been. The successful involvement in the Youth Training Scheme has beenn useful in clearly demonstrating how people are able to respond to learning opportunities. Quite junior employees have contributed to the training of the youth trainees, which has increased expectations of how the Bank should provide facilities for learning, and work-based learning in particular.

5   Results and achievements

The Bank's training policy is undergoing a fundamental review. One of the stimuli for this is the comprehensive review of the scheme of classification of banking jobs which guides career advancement and salary progression. The overall objective of the review, which is being conducted in a consultative manner, is to update the job relationships and grade hierarchy introduced in 1979 so that it better fits today's requirements. The revised scheme is also expected to: '. . .act as a springboard for important changes in attitudes of mind, with the accent on fulfilment of potential giving way to the achievement of a high level of performance'. This statement in the notice to staff, describing the results of the discussions to formulate the proposals for the new scheme and the work that still needs to be done, very clearly sets out the precepts which guide the reasoning upon which the proposals are founded. They illustrate how 'continuous development' activity for people can fit into the continuing development of the business:

(i)   The Bank of England, as a Central Bank, needs to ensure a high standard of performance in its work.

(ii) The Bank's role in the economy requires it not only to possess qualities of dependability and stability, but also to be responsive to change.

(iii) To fulfil this role, the Bank needs a staffing structure which is flexible and adaptable.

(iv) Staff resources are the Bank's most important asset and, to develop these to the full, the Bank needs to give appropriate emphasis to training and development and to delegation of responsibility.

(v)   Remuneration should be more directly related to individual performance and, for this and other reasons, staff should be subject to regular and objective assessment.

The four proposed levels – entry and support staff; the

professional group and management; senior officials; and directors – imply, amongst many other important considerations, revised bases for career progression and the provision and management of training and development. The mechanisms for promotion are being reviews, and an assessment centre approach is being considered; and it is intended that the appraisal system will be strengthened.

Any serious reconsideration of how people are managed demands care that the best of the past is maintained as well as introducing new policies and practices. The Bank appreciates the contribution which continuous development of its people will make. To quote from an internal training policy paper: 'The costs of training. . .are seen . . . as an investment, rather than as an extravagance'.

It is an investment which is paying and should continue to pay dividends.

10 Noble Lowndes and Partners Limited
Continuous development within the pensions industry

1 Background data

For over fifty years Noble Lowndes has been at the forefront of the development of occupational pensions schemes. In 1969 it became part of the Hill Samuel Group, the financial services organization, and, since 1979 when it was reformed into a separate autonomous company within the Group, it has established itself as market leader in employee benefits services in terms of both revenue and number of clients.

Worldwide, the company has over 5,000 corporate and 70,000 private clients. Its corporate clients include one in four of 'The Times Top 1,000' companies in the UK and one in four of the 'Fortune 500' in the USA.

Amongst its services it provides employee benefits consultancy, actuarial consultancy, personal financial services and pensions administration throughout the UK, and in the USA, Australasia and Europe.

In 1985–6 the company earned a pre-tax profit of £8.5 million on a turnover of £44 million.

There has been considerable investment in computer systems to support the business during a period from 1979 when staff numbers have grown worldwide from about 1,000 people to nearly 1,500 in 1986.

It is absolutely essential for the company not only to anticipate pressures and changes in its market-places, but also to be alert and respond rapidly to legislative change. Both in the UK and elsewhere, governments intervene with financial, tax and regulatory measures which have powerful impacts upon the sort of services which may be offered, and on the needs of clients.

The market-place itself, domestically and internationally, has become intensely competitive. Existing business needs to be protected by excellent service and new business can be obtained only by demonstrating the highest professional standards and efficiency. Clients are very discerning and value for money is a critical consideration.

Continuing success, as a result, demands a flexible, responsive organization and a versatile, highly skilled and committed staff who recognize that their capabilities require frequent enhancement.

Noble Lowndes' services are continually developing, so continuous development for its staff is vital. It has been recognized for a long time that it is just as important to use the business to grow the people as it is to use the people to grow the business, particularly as, in essence, it is a knowledge-based enterprise.

2   Policy/philosophy

In a very real sense, Noble Lowndes is in the business of education. Much of its promotion to prospective clients and much of its service to clients is the provision of information, the updating of knowledge, assisting understanding, influencing values and attitudes, helping people to evaluate priorities and to make decisions. Communicating effectively with corporate bodies and private individuals is a key activity within most of the job in the company.

A typical consultant or client service technician has to possess considerable knowledge of a number of highly complicated financial topics and, what is more, explain them to lay people!

Traditionally in the industry, most recruits started their careers in pensions administration: the natural place to gain a sound understanding of the intricacies of the subject and the starting point for a career in itself. Everybody was encouraged to make progress and everybody got the same chance of promotion. Advancement was, however, almost entirely by individual effort.

But for many years, reflecting the considerable complexity of the business and its ever-increasing demands for new knowledge and skill, Noble Lowndes has adopted a more coherent and planned approach to the development of people. Whilst the same career routes are still open to everyone and individual effort is still essential, there is a deliberate policy of recruiting highly able, energetic people, many of them graduates, who can assimilate complex information, re-learn rapidly and who can innovate and cope with a physically, as well as intellectually, demanding life-style. It is still a high effort, high achievement, high reward business.

Against this background, the company's emphasis upon education and training is even more highly visible to its staff. The strong support and encouragement for learning is managed not as 'extraordinary' or 'bolted on' but so that it will be actively accepted by the staff as an integral part of the company culture. It is a knowledge-based business for clients and staff alike.

But skilled, well rewarded, professional people are often 'loners'. Individual competence is essential but not sufficient for success in the employee benefits business. High quality service to clients demands high quality team-work amongst groups of technical specialists. So besides being capable within their own spheres of expertise, the staff have to appreciate other people's expertise to be able to collaborate effectively. Because of this there is considerable emphasis throughout the company upon interdependence and team work. The concept of the team pervades company documentation and communication.

THE REGIONAL TEAM

BOARD OF DIRECTORS OF CUBIE WOOD & CO LTD

REGIONAL DIRECTOR Director of NL Pensions Ltd

SALES DIRECTOR Director of NL Pensions Ltd

ASSISTANT REGIONAL DIRECTOR

REGIONAL ACTUARY

REGIONAL CONSULTANT

Team responsible for:
- Assignments for new or prospective clients

ADMINISTRATION MANAGER

ASSISTANT ACTUARY

Team responsible for:
- Actuarial Advice
- Valuations
- Statistical Investigations
- Transfer Factors

TECHNICAL MANAGER

Team responsible for:
- Trust Documentation
- Scheme Rules
- Explanatory Booklets
- Inland Revenue negotiations
- Research & Development

ACCOUNT MANAGERS

Responsible for:
- Consultancy
- Trustee services
- Communication
- Risk management advice

CENTRAL SERVICES

- Central Research Department
- Axon Communications (special communication assignments)
- Investment Performance Monitoring Service
- Noble Lowndes Benefit Consultants Ltd (employee share schemes)

ADMINISTRATION CONTROLLERS

Team responsible for:
- Administration
- Trustee Records
- Calculations
- Payments

REGIONAL SYSTEMS CONTROLLER

Team responsible for:
- Computer-based Administration, Actuarial & Accounting Systems
- Word processing

REGIONAL FUND ACCOUNTANT

Team responsible for:
- Pension Scheme Accounts
- Cashiering & Management Accounting

The Chief Executive's report in 1986 demonstrates this:

. . .our prosperity must be based upon strong sales and servicing teams.

It is to the great credit of the team as a whole that those involved [in senior management changes] were able to take on their additional responsibilities confident that they had the full support of all their colleagues at every level.

. . .corporate achievements are a reflection of the people in the team and their will to succeed at whatever they do.

This sentiment is reflected not only in the approach to people development, but also in the structure of the organization and in the approaches to managing and developing people.

In the UK the principal operation, corporate services, is decentralized, with regional offices in major cities in England and Scotland. Each office provides a full range of services through teams of actuaries, technicians, consultants and sales specialists. These teams are supported by administration, systems and accounting groups.

In such a geographically widely spread organization, it is not possible to provide adequately for people development on a centralized basis, even it it were desirable. So the company operates with a small central core of specialist training staff who liaise with regional training co-ordinators – typically senior managers who have training as one of their major responsibilities.

The structure is simple:

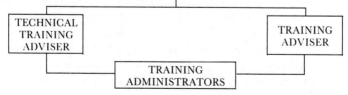

DIRECTOR PERSONNEL AND
MANAGEMENT SERVICES
TRAINING MANAGER
TRAINING SERVICES MANAGER

TECHNICAL
TRAINING
ADVISER

TRAINING
ADVISER

TRAINING
ADMINISTRATORS

Influential though the central Training Services Department is, the Training Programme Booklet which the department publishes every two years or so reminds everyone of where the greatest accountability lies:

> Although the responsibility for the training and development of staff rests with Regional/Departmental Management, the Training Services Department exists to provide a specialist service, giving advice and practical assistance, to enable regional training requirements to be satisfied.

The assistance include analysis of training needs, design of training, choice of methods, planning and provision of equipment.

The Department, in addition, organizes a number of company-wide courses – a three-stage induction, communication skills, a suite of integrated management and supervisory modules (people and team skills being prominent amongst them), personal skills such as creative thinking and time management and, as would be expected in a client-orientated business, selling skills and technical pensions programmes. The instructions for nominations for the courses and the emphasis on pre-course briefing and post-course review again places responsibility with the line management and plays its part in ensuring that the learning relates realistically to the current and future job roles of the participants.

The Further Education Policy is similarly published:

> Noble Lowndes and Partners believe that young persons setting out on a career within the company should fit themselves for advancement by studying for a professional qualification directly relevant to their careers.

Encouragement to invest time and effort in study includes financial support, study time and coaching and advice, and financial rewards on successful completion.

Whilst the emphasis is upon Pensions Management, Actuarial and Insurance education which the company encourages as a means of expanding the individual's knowledge and widening the perspective in which their technical expertise is understood, sponsorship is available for other study which is relevant to the job being done. It also encourages GCSE, 'A' level and BTEC National Certificate study as a means of admittance to professional education courses.

The philosophy which lies behind the practice is quite clearly that staff should develop their competence to provide a high quality of service to the clients. The company does much to encourage self development by providing a climate in which skill and achievement are the basis for advancement and the means for learning.

Nowhere is this more clearly demonstrated than in the Pensions Administrator Skill Scheme (PASS) which lays the foundation for continuous development for many of the staff and which leads on to a Personal Development Programme (PDP) as the individual's career progresses.

3   Continuous development practice

3.1   *Responsibilities and roles*

Each new pensions administrator is issued with a comprehensive Trainee Log. It is a development plan which details the knowledge and skills which have to be acquired if the recruit is to become fully competent. The knowledge and skills are described in operating, or performance, terms and the required attainments have been systematically analysed and grouped into a six-level hierarchy reflecting the typical (but not necessarily the only) sequence in which the corresponding job tasks and responsibilities are likely to be taken on. The purposes of the Log are to 'recognize and reward increasing proficiency' and to provide a sort of route map for encouraging and directing progressive achievement in job performance.

The Managing Director's introductory note in the document reaffirms the company commitment to on-the-job development and the expectation it has of the newcomer that he or she is the person most responsible for the learning.

As he puts it, the skills described in the Log are those which '. . .we shall expect you to acquire through both on-the-job and off-the-job training'. What the company has provided is 'a structured framework' and pay increases related to success at each of the six levels. These payments are in addition to the annual salary reviews and are another unambiguous signal of the value placed upon expertise.

The company also provides a trainer, who perhaps could be more appropriately called a mentor: typically the boss of the trainee pensions administrator. The role of the trainer is to help to plan and organize the training, both on-the-job and off-the-job, with the trainee and ensure that the learning objectives are achieved in due course. Progress is regularly assessed and trainees carefully counselled as necessary. When a particular learning object-ive has been achieved, the trainer signs it off in the Log.

There is back-up support to the trainer and trainee from the local Administration Manager or Training Co-ordinator and from time to time the Training Log is reviewed by a Regional Manager.

These 'lay' trainers are not left to muddle their way through their mentor role. The Training Services Depart-ment provides a one-day training skills module which assists understanding and practice of individual coaching and a further two-day training skills module on group instructional techniques.

3.2   *Identification of learning opportunities and needs*

The PASS approach, it is important to point out, runs alongside any professional education such as for the Pensions Management Institute qualifications. (Every-one is encouraged to undertake the study but there is no insistence that the exams are taken.) The PASS, much of the learning within which is on-the-job, and the profes-sional study are seen as complementary.

The main feature of the Log is the six skill levels which are expected to be achieved by a typical trainee over a period of approximately three years. Within each level are the generic needs which have been identified for the key activities of the pensions administrator role. The pace, and indeed the sequence, of learning for a particular individual is determined not only by the experience which he or she brings as a recruit and his or her ability to learn, but also by what can be provided in the work itself. So against the background of an overall training plan, the trainee and trainer plot a particular route which is possible and suitable. In this way the individual's specific needs may be addressed.

The main vehicle for ensuring that this happens is the preparation, within the Log, of a monthly project plan. This is done by the trainer and agreed with the trainee. The plan identifies the activities and learning aims for the next period. For each, the method of learning to be used (such as a reading assignment, course attendance or on-the-job coaching) is specified together with the date by which the aims are expected to be achieved.

The plan acts as a reference and record to steer and note the trainee's learning and it forms the basis for the preparation by the trainee of a progress report on achievement towards the end of each month.

So each month, work-related learning aims are specified, plans are laid for their achievement – principally through the work activity – progress is reviewed and the learning aims updated. Trainees expect and are expected to learn most by doing their work under guidance. Moreover the learning is expected to be continuous and orderly. Opportunities, as well as demands for acquiring further competence arise or can be created in the job. Learning is anchored in the work, it arises obviously and essentially from the work and its achievement is clearly demonstrable in enhanced working competence.

3.3 *Learner involvement*

The possession and frequent use of the Training Log focuses the involvement of the trainee in the training. Not only does the learner participate fully in identifying learning requirements and in specifying how they might be fulfilled, but he or she is required to compile regularly a report on progress. At the end of each week, the trainee is asked to reflect upon and describe on a record sheet in the Log what has been done and what has been learned, by what method and, interestingly, from whom. (It is recognized in the company that there is a general responsibility to help others to learn.) These weekly notes are summarized at the end of the month in terms of significant learning, work achievements and what has been of most interest. Trainees are encouraged to describe any new learning needs or aspirations which have been revealed or stimulated by the experiences ot the past month.

The trainer reads, adds comments to the report and uses it during the regular review discussions.

This device ensures the continuity of one learning phase with another and the frequency of the reporting and discussing, discussing and planning, planning and doing, reporting and discussing cycle reinforces the naturalness of progressive learning within the job. The trainee is not just involved in learning as 'trainee' but also as 'worker'. The company underlines this by rewarding financially the 'worker' at intervals as the competence develops further.

3.4   *Learning resources*

The main resource is the capability of the learner to learn, and the work he or she is given to do.

The company makes available its own internal programmes, external education and training programmes and uses consultants within the company as necessary. Current demand exceeds the capacity and ways are being sought to expand facilities particularly by means of open-learning approaches. However, in what might be termed the 'post professional apprenticeship' stage, the emphasis within the company is even more upon personal (and continuous) development.

Each senior pensions administrator has a Personal Development Log and it is used in a similar way as in the PASS, but with even more emphasis upon self development. The development objectives are in further technical expertise and in supervisory and managerial capabilities. The Log guides the learner through a pool of possible learning assignments, coaching sessions, exercises, courses, specified reading, work experience, as well as personal development planning guides.

At the end of each three months the learner meets with the Administration Manager to review progress and plan the next quarter's learning assignments. Learner involvement in the management of the learningg process is encouraged by requiring the pensions administrator to compose a quarterly reiew of activities and achievements which also provides an opportunity to look ahead and plan for the next period.

An individual development programme lasting two days is available to assist senior administration and technical staff to help them to appreciate how their performance might be improved and what skills they will need to acquire for promotion to consultancy roles. It is conducted similarly to an Assessment Centre with group and individual exercises but with guidance and counselling based upon the outcomes.

As senior administrators advance into management positions, their individual development needs are met by a blend of internal and external courses. But the expectation remains that they should continue to learn, and learn actively, from their meetings and conferences within the company and not least from working closely with clients.

4   Problems

Noble Lowndes is a very successful business, and training within it has made a considerable contribution to that success. However, the major problems, as training has become an accepted, natural feature of the company's everyday activity, have arisen largely out of the company's success.

Business growth brings a constant demand for people at all levels in all roles to upgrade knowledge and skills. But the growth and the need to continue to provide high quality service increases workload and pressures upon time. Time is precious and is more likely to be devoted to getting the job done well than grasping the learning opportunity. It is certainly not easy to release people for off-the-job training, however beneficial it might be.

Growth often brings skill and experience shortages and, as a result, it is not always possible to promote from within to senior or specialist positions even when highly desirable. Paradoxically, good training and continuous development arouse expectations of continuous advancement which sometimes cannot be fulfilled. Ensuring that development and career progression are congruent is difficult, and the problem can be aggravated because costs of moving people on promotion from one region to another, particularly to the South East of England, are prohibitive.

It is a serious concern because, as many other companies which take training seriously have found, Noble Lowndes' well trained staff are very attractive to predatory competitors!

The other problem arising from the success of the training is that as demand for assistance from the Training Services Department exceeds capacity, a feeling may be aroused that not enough is being done.

5   Results and achievements

Training and development is acknowledged as part of the Nobl Lowndes way of life. It is viewed as vital for ensuring competence in the present job and essential for progression into more demanding roles. The staff appreciate that the responsibility for self development is theirs, and that what the company must do, and indeed all it can do, is to provide opportunity, facilities and guidance.

It is well understood that it is professional competencce which determines the quality of service to clients and therefore the overall success of the business. The prosperity of the company and of its staff depends upon its competitive edge and, in a knowledge-based industry, that demands continuing development of high-calibre people.

The responsibility for training lies with the responsibility for performance: in the line. Not only is responsibility for training widely accepted, but responsibility in *actively* training is recognized by most managers and supervisors.

The first test of achievement is whether or not all the effort ensures the people requirements of the business are satisfied. Internal promotion is satisfactory, a very high proportion of able people are retained and enjoy fulfilling careers over long periods. And the continued growth (in revenue, profit, market share and the acquisition of new prestigious clients) is the ultimate test.

The major lesson which Noble Lowndes' experience demonstrates is that investment in training pays off in business results. But to maintain business results demands maintaining the training effort. In a market which rapidly changes and where the organization must respond swiftly to threat and opportunity, the people must be flexible and responsive. They must be skilled and expert learners as well as skilled and expert employee benefits professionals. An orderly systematic programme of work-based learning has promoted this learning attitude.

Because the foundations have been well laid, apart from more closely relating recruitment and training policy and practice, the way ahead lies primarily in establishing more and even better training facilities. Attention is being given to involving the overseas operations more closely in the training activity, and more is being done to integrate the business monitoring and service department processes with the training, particularly for consultants. When this is achieved, the development activity will demonstrate even more powerfully the effectiveness of the company's approach to continuous development.

11 Austin Rover
Continuous development within the motor industry

1 Background data

Austin Rover is one of the three product companies within the Rover Group plc – the others are Land Rover and

Freight Rover (Leyland Trucks having been recently sold). Some 99.7% of the ordinary share capital of Rover Group is held by the Secretary of State for Trade and Industry. Sales revenue in 1986 was around £3,400 million of which £1,100 million was earned overseas. Direct exports from the UK are valued at about £800 million per annum.

The Group employs 60,000 people in the UK and the 2,000 component supplier companies and 1,000 dealerships employ about 190,000 people.

Austin Rover itself is the largest indigenous UK manufacturer of motor cars and car-derived vans. It produces over half of all the cars made in Britain. Its own sales revenue is over £2,200 million a year of which £350 million is export sales to over 40 countries. Its range includes Rover 800, Rover 200, Mini, Metro, Maestro and 17 Montego models. It also makes bodies for Rolls Royce.

Some 39,000 people are employed in the 12 main factories in Wales, the Midlands, Leeds, Swindon and Oxford. It is the continuous development (CD) activity at the Cowley Body Plant which this case example describes.

2   Policy/philosophy

Two factors will continue to determine the success of the business:

(i) the exploitation of the most modern technology in the research and development required for the design and manufacture of new models, and its application in production

(ii) the further enhancement of the skills and the effective direction of the efforts of the workforce.

The very latest computer-aided engineering and flexible manufacturing systems involving robotics are used to ensure:

- speedier development of new models
- greater efficiency in production
- increased quality and reliability for the customer.

Indeed, production improvements already match or exceed the best in Europe. But there is no illusion that the technology can achieve all that is required without the most substantial contribution from the people.

As stated in the publication 'Austin Rover and New Technology', produced by the External Affairs Department:

> . . .[Austin Rover] has developed processes in which the skills of employees combine with robotics and automated systems to create some of the most modern production lines in the motor industry.

The technology and the people are essentially, mutually supportive.

> With robots taking over many of the repetitive and uncongenial tasks there is a higher degree of responsibility and job satisfaction for the shop-floor employees.

However, these demands for new skills and competence to fulfil the growing responsibilities are not restricteedd to the shop-floor and are not once-and-for-all. Rover Group Chairman, Mr Graham Day, stated at the 1987 Institute of Directors' Annual Convention:

> The proccess of acquiring 'add on', 'top-up' or totally new skills cannot be viewed as a one-off exercise. Indeed the time is close upon us when, for the most part, skills enhancement must become an ongoing process in the normal course of employment. . .The continuing need for re-skilling, or whatever other label we may choose to attach to the acquisition of fresh or additional skills, is not confined to manual workers, technicians, office support staff or people in specialist employment. In industry and business this need extends also to managers.

Austin Rover places great emphasis upon promotion from within and this also reinforces the need to provide a climate which encourages learning and real opportunities for career progression and advancement, particularly from the shop floor.

There is a clearly specified, written policy for training and development and manuals to guide its implementation. The policy and practices acknowledge that the payoff which most people seek from their work is no longer restricted to money as it might have been under piece-rate payment systems. They wish to be involved in their work, they wish to use their talents and they value genuine interest being taken in them and in their contribution to the business. So, for the company, training is promoted as very much an integral part of working. It supports the people who conduct the business activity. As a result it is fundamentally line managers' responsibility to ensure that people are capable of performing well and do perform well. Managers are responsible for their own development and for guiding that of those they lead. In a company where even the most senior of managers is highly visible to the workforce and meets formally and informally with them regularly, training and development is a key emphasis. The clear expectation is that:

- people need and will continue to develop further competence

- standards of performance and achievement will continue to improve

- opportunities and facilities to encourage development will continue to be provided.

3   Continuous development practice

3.1   *Responsibilities and roles*

With this approach to human resource development, the company is able to rely upon a small number of training specialists to provide expert advice and some of the training activity where it is appropriate. At Cowley one Training Manager (who also carries out resource allocation of hourly paid employees) looks after the manufacturing training, a second looks after staff training and a third manager concentrates upon employee development.

They, in turn, receive assistance from the Training Director and his colleagues (based at the Haseley Manor Training Centre), for example with the design of training material.

The training staff are purposely shifting the emphasis away from providing training towards encouraging managers to recognize learning needs and opportunities in and near the workplace and towards supporting local training initiatives.

Other important responsibilities of the training staff include monitoring the effectiveness of training, reviewing programmes and providing expert assistance to managers in a variety of work group discussion meetings.

3.2 *Identification of learning opportunities and needs*

Managers and supervisors are expected to be close enough to their teams to be able to identify individuals with potential for progression. There is, as the Manufacturing Manager expresses it, 'a constant look-out for talent'. But it is no hit-or-miss affair. Managers are regularly asked to nominate candidates for promotion to supervisor. Nominees participate in a supervisors' Assessment Centre where not only are existing attributes determined but learning needs also identified. Successful candidates are 'followed through' on the succession plan which is typically reviewed each month. This process is complemented by the 'trainability testing' of hourly paid workers such as metal finishers and welders to establish their skill and foremanship potential. The selection of superintendents is assisted by a similar Assessment Centre process. But again the identification of potential and learning needs is not left to these more formal mechanisms. The appraisal system is expected to identify development needs, nominated people are interviewed and their progression reviewed by senior executives, all candidates for promotion are interviewed by the Production Manager and all graduates are interviewed at least once a year. Working experience and performance records are carefully reviewed and play just as important a part in forming the views about an individual as the formal Assessment Centre does.

This close involvement of managers in the assessment, progression and guidance of their people, and the open manner in which it is conducted, demonstrate the company's commitment to the development of its workforce. This demonstration starts for the hourly paid worker with the five and a half day induction course, involving not only the new starters themselves but also their families. It is a vitally important ingredient in promoting care for the quality of the work done and the products which are produced.

Perhaps the clearest example of this thoughtful and carefully planned approach to anchoring the learning to the requirements of the work is the preparation undertaken for the manufacture of the XX Model (which became the Rover 800). The foremen for the new production plant were carefully selected, they were inducted into their new roles, they participated in the design of the new workplaces and their facilities, and they were systematically and regularly briefed about the progress being made in preparing for the introduction of the new cars. The training programmes, which were led entirely by senior managers themselves, raised competence in interpersonal skills, problem sharing and communicating, and helped to orientate the supervisors for their new roles. The hourly paid employees on the Rover 800 production also received one week's induction.

So the learning needs arose from the business and the business activity itself provided the locus and the focus for the learning.

3.3   Learner involvement

The Austin Rover approach to development is not piecemeal and neither is it superficial not 'bolt-on' to the main thrusts of the company. Development and training are an integral part of the managing processes. Indeed, some of the learning which is encouraged would hardly be recognized as a training activity because it is so naturally a part of the way eveyday things are done. For example, the plant has a monthly briefing group 'cascade' system by which the Operations Director keeps his senior team informed; they then pass on information to their teams so that eventually foremen, having been briefed by their superintendents, are able to keep the shop-floor employees in touch with important company matters. Each stage is, of course, a two-way communication process and the way people react and respond is carefully considered. The briefings also provide the opportunity to ensure that local news and views are exchanged. This is one means of ensuring people have the opportunity to be involved in matters affecting them, and the surveys of the effectiveness of the briefings which are undetaken from time to time, provide additional, important information about what improvements might need to be made. The knowledge exchange is only one of the benefits. Communication skills can be enhanced, understanding of the challenges to and the priorities for the company and the contributions required from everyone are a vital support to a CD development approach.

But there is a great deal which can only be learned from doing the work itself. Much of the work in production is organized into 'zones'. Groups of 25 to 30 people are responsible for organizing, planning and controlling their work. They can call upon specialized help when it is needed. These working groups are supported by 'Zone Circles': something like quality circles but with a concentration upon developing teamwork and presentation skills as well as problem solving and specialized matters like inventory control. The supervisors who lead the circles have been trained to do so. Problems are identified and contributions to solving them are sought. But in the ten hours or so which is the minimum total time the several meetings take the emphasis is on learning.

Indeed, these zone circles are one element in a more broadly conceived 'working with pride' programme into which much of the development effort is incorporated, especially that related to team skills. In addition there is an Employee Involvement Programme which includes 'think tanks to find ways of reducing production costs' and a Young People's Advisory Panel drawn from across the company, which contributes to the design process. Again, learning is primarily by tackling real problems and by making a worthwhile contribution to the business.

Austin Rover has been a strong innovator and supporter of open learning and has provided facilities at Longbridge and Haseley Manor as well as at Cowley. This reinforces the emphasis on learners being responsible for their own learning.

One final example of involving people in determining what they need to learn and do is the use of the 'Audit Bay'. Every day a sample of no less than fourteen cars are taken from the end of the line and everything checked from a customer's point of view in the audit bay. People from the production areas are taken to see the examinations taking place, and, each day, the Plant Director, the manufacturing managers and superintendents pay a visit. This not only focuses continually upon the quality standards required, but fosters the pride in achievement so necessary for standards to be maintained and, indeed, improved. Everyone is able to recognize the final outcome of the individual effort and application of individual skill and the team-work which Austin Rover people believe encourages further learning.

3.4   *Learning resources*

It is not really the open learning facilities, Haseley Manor, the small number of training specialists and some carefully designed programmes – such as the 13-week foremen's course, or the two-week middle-managers' course – which represent the learning resources of the company. The company takes more conventional training activity seriously, even to the extent of promoting a customer care programme for the 10,000 staff in its 1,300 dealer network.

The anticipation of and responsiveness to change in the business requirements are part of the strength. The work itself is the key stimulus to learning – it is the work which is required to be done which highlights the learning needs and it is the preparation for and the doing of the work which satisfies those needs. This doesn't mean that off-the-job programmes are devalued. Recently an Outward Bound course was chosen to enhance team-work across plant boundaries for example. But so much can be and is being achieved by selected placements in various departments and guided experience, by carefully supervised work-based project work and similar means.

4   Problems

Such a continuous approach to human resource development is by no means all plain sailing. Like almost every other business in viciously competitive markets, there are never enough hours in the day or money available for Austin Rover to do all it would like to do. Getting the work out – finished, high quality, vehicles off the line – is the major preoccupation of manager and managed alike. So even the good, imaginative training idea might be, from time to time, accepted but not implemented.

Open learning seems indisputably a good idea. But is it for people who work hard and long, and who need to get away from the workplace for a while and unwind?

In spite of all the concern, the care and the effort, the feeling is that the relating of learning and development to career progression is still too crude and inexact.

Despite all the professional expertise which goes into the design and delivery of courses, work experience and all the other development activity, it is still felt that validation and demonstration of the benefits are inadequate.

And, finally, of course, not everyone welcomes the emphasis on continuing developmeent, responding to change, preparing for new challenges. There is still much to be done before the overwhelming majority of employees (at all levels) not only appreciate their need to continue to enhance their capabilities, but are enthusiastic about the prospect of undertaking the necessary steps to achieve it.

5   Results and achievements

But much more than a start has been made. Particularly

amongst senior managers and directors, there is a commitment to the development of the workforce because it is fundamental to the achievement of the business objectives. New training initiatives are welcomed. Among the workforce at large there is a growing understanding of and co-operation with training: participants on courses for example report favourably on their experience. So, just as the methods of selecting for promotion have been improved, the preparation of people for promotion continues to improve, and this is seen more and more as a naturally continuing process.

More broadly there is a movement away from a narrow, task orientation towards a more open-thinking, imaginative organization – and this is by no means restricted to senior levels. It has less to do with making cars than with recognizing and fulfilling the customers' wishes.

What is more, the evidence of this expanding vision is to be seen in the improvement in the quality and reputation of the products. The daily quality audits indicate it, and so do the quality tracking surveys with customers. The company is viewed, more than ever before, in the words of the Manufacturing Manager, as 'a reliable, volume producer at a sensible price'.

Much has been accomplished, and much has been learned by those involved, which will help to achieve much of what is still to do.

Leading by strong example has been one foundation of the success so far. Managers, even though they have specific and particular responsibilities, have also a more general responsibility for the operation. If their staff are to broaden their vision, they have to demonstrate what is required in their own behaviour. The expectations they have of their staff have parallels in the expectations their staff have of them. Managers set the cultural tone and climate.

But even the setting of example and the encouragement of participation and involvement in the important activities of the company do not lead to change overnight. There is conservatism and even scepticism still to be overcome. Different people learn differently and at different rates. Not everyone is inspired by the same activity or opportunity. So there is a need to mount and maintain a variety of initiatives supporting the same approach. The initiatives should reinforce each other, each a variation on a theme but a consistent theme nevertheless. The changing of attitudes and the enhancement of capabilities require time, so those who lead the changes need patience, resilience and persistence.

The style now seems well established. Whilst there will be continuing attention to improving still further the various courses which are provided, and introducing, for example, a superintendents' programme similar to the 13-week foremen course, much of the attention will be given to tailor-making learning to the particular needs of individuals and the business. There will not be prescribed courses for everyone. So the training specialists are likely to focus upon how better to clarify and specify learning needs, and to assist line managers and supervisors to do so and then provide appropriate learning opportunities.

All this effort will be directed towards meeting the major business challenges, including satisfying customer wants, further improvement in efficiency and increasing penetration in selected markets.

As Mr Day said in his Institute of Directors address:

> We should never take the view that the training or retraining of people is an altruistic undertaking. The current focus on re-skilling is properly prompted by enlightened self interest.

The CD efforts of Austin Rover have been successful so far – energy costs have been halved in recent years and materials costs held down. Productivity increased from just under 7 cars per employee per year in 1980 to 12 in 1983.

A quarter of the 500,000 cars and vans produced are exported.

Continuous development is helping to link the proud past to the exciting future.

12   Grow South!
Continuous development in a local collaborative project

1   Background data

Grow South! is the collaborative project for South Bank development and training. It is one of over 400 Local Collaborative Projects (LCPs) which have been set up throughout mainland Britain, funded by the Department of Education and Science and the Manpower Services Commission. Simply, LCPs are attempts by consortia of college and employer representatives to investigate and make plans to satisfy the training needs of a local community. Having set the ball rolling, it is intended that the work begun by LCPs will be self-perpetuating and self-financing. Each LCP is thus granted only a limited life. Grow South! has a year to do its work.

Its two full-time and two part-time staff are based at South Bank Technopark, itself an 'incubator unit' for high tech firms. Technopark is a separate company of the South Bank Polytechnic receiving financial backing from the Prudential. Unlike most LCPs, Grow South! is not industry specific. Grow South! began its operations in August 1986 and was due to complete its work in July 1987. The DES is Grow South!'s treasurer; the scheme has been awarded a total grant of £52,000. Obligations which must be fulfilled include the analysis of the training needs of the local community and the organization of pilot programmes to meet needs shown to be priorities.

Grow South! has some features in common with any other large-scale LCP, but rather a lot that are not!

2   Responsibilities and roles

Grow South!'s board of directors is its Steering Group, formed by collaborative partners together with representatives of the funding bodies. Each collaborative partner has agreed to contribute the equivalent of £5,000 pa for three years to fund Grow South! Collaborative partners include: IBM, Charles Barker, Arthur Young, the National

Theatre, NHS, London Chamber of Commerce, Network Southeast, Charles Letts. The team is constantly on the look-out for new partners to join the venture.

The Director of Grow South! reports to the Steering Group.

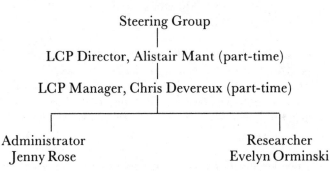

Steering Group
|
LCP Director, Alistair Mant (part-time)
|
LCP Manager, Chris Devereux (part-time)

Administrator   Researcher
Jenny Rose   Evelyn Orminski

The relationship between the Director and Manager of Grow South! is analogous to the relationship between a company chairman and managing director. The four staff work together as a team and divide the responsibilities of running the LCP through a system of regular team meetings at which short-term goals are decided and tasks allocated against time limits. The team is aware of its responsibility to learn new things in response to the emerging needs of clients. Like many another small group, members of the team are aware of the need to manage contingencies and to make small incremental steps today both to meet contingencies and to make possible the achievement of the longer term goals of tomorrow. Members of the team are themselves conscious of being continuous learners.

3   Policy and philosophy

The team's aim is to help people, especially in small firms:

- to recognize what they are good at and what they need to be good at, now and later
- to encourage intra- and inter-firm team building and team working (to allow individuals to learn

from one another and to exercise their own special talents)
- to spot development opportunities (not excluding formal education and training)
- to perceive these things as so obvious and natural that self directed learning activity becomes entrenched.

In these ways they hope to assist organizations to grow and/or prosper in order to develop the local economy or the services provided. It is the Grow South! team's goal that at the end of the LCP's life, a continuing, self-help learning group will have evolved to take its place.

4   The identification of learning needs

Like any other LCP management team, Grow South! personnel set out to analyse the training needs in a locality. Their first problem was to define the boundaries of the

Figure 1: The ten regions of Grow South!

locality; not a straightforward task in an inner city area. It was advisable also not to encroach upon the territories of other inner city project teams. Delineating Grow South!'s boundaries was achieved by constructing a map of the district within 20 minutes' walk of the project's base at the Elephant and Castle. The data gathered were based on local people's perceived notion of the area they either lived or worked in rather than postal or administrative boundaries. Key roads proved to be large perceptual barriers and effectively defined the limit of the southern margin of the 'patch'. The river formed the natural northern boundary.

Having defined the area, the team investigated what it contained. The data shown on the figure which follows were obtained from the appropriate land use survey. Grow South! territory is remarkable in that it contains a vast number of organizations in a few square miles; whilst most of the organizations are tiny (1-5 person operations), the area includes 14 of the Times Top 1,000 companies.

Figure 2: Distribution of 5,037 firms in Grow South! region

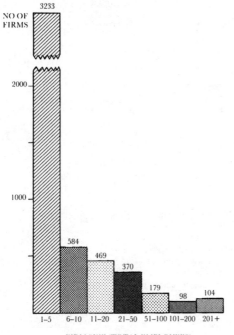

FIRM SIZE (TOTAL EMPLOYEES)

The next logical step was to find out what business the 5,000 were in. The breakdown is best shown diagrammatically. The figure which follows shows the *major* functions of the organizations in each class according to size. The numbers in the pie charts refer to the standard industrial classification (SIC) code numbers (definitions are shown in the key).

Figure 3: Major functions of firms in each class

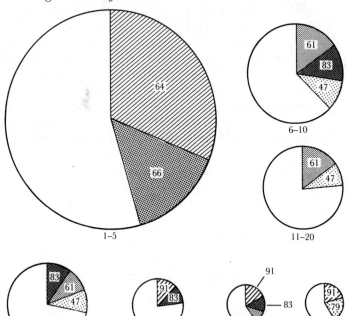

KEY
47   Manufacture of paper, printing and publishing
61   Wholesale distribution
64   Retail distribution
66   Hotels and catering
79   Postal services and telecommunications
83   Business services
91   Public administration

1–5 (etc) = size of firm
Circles proportional to number of firms in each class size.

Of the 53 major industrial classifications in the Grow South! region, seven stand out as being representative of a particular size of firm or the total population of firms, as follows:

Figure 4: Major firm classifications

The numbers and text are taken from the Central Statistical Office's 'Standard Industrial Classification, Revised 1980', published by HMSO.

47	Manufacture of paper, printing and publishing	
61	Wholesale distribution	Industrial materials, timber and building materials, household goods, textiles, clothing, food, drink and pharmaceutical products
64	Retail distribution	Food retailing, confectioners, tobacconists, newsagents, off-licences, chemists, retail distribution of clothing and footwear, household goods, hardware and ironmongery
66	Hotels and catering	Hotels and guest houses, restaurants, snack bars, cafes, public houses
79	Postal services and telecommunications	
83	Business services	Estate agents, legal services, accountants, advertising, computer services
91	Public administration	National and local government services, Justice, Police, fire services, national defence, social security.

The Grow South! team considered this early concentration on analysis vital to decision making. The data allowed the team to see clearly where their efforts should be concentrated. Evidently, particular attention needed to be focused on small firms (see Figure 1: 62% of firms employ 1–5 people, largely in retail distribution and catering). Many of the very large organizations had been found to be in the 'people processing' business, a third in public administration. There are two large hospitals, two major railway stations, an arts complex, a number of educational institutions and many hotels and restaurants. Seemingly therefore, developing first-rate customer care and customer service were obvious and natural needs. The 'business' of the large firms is indicated below:

Figure 5: Major classifications of large firms
(200+ employees)

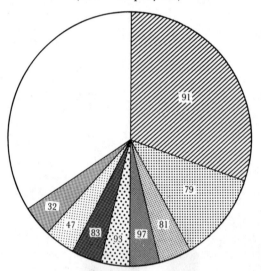

KEY

		%	No. of organizations
91	Public administration	30.8	32
79	Postal services and telecommunications	10.6	11
81	Banking and finance	5.8	6
97	Recreational services and other cultural services	4.8	5
93	Education	4.8	5
83	Business services	4.8	5
47	Manufacture of paper, printing and publishing	4.8	5
32	Mechanical engineering	4.8	5
		71.2	74

5   Continuous development practice

The Director and Manager of Grow South! began their work by visiting organizations, large and small, in the categories identified as predominant in the locality, to explain what the LCP was about and to discuss how it could act as a middleman in assisting the organization to solve those problems susceptible to a training solution. The interviewers, through questioning, listening and observing, sought to help interviewees to think:

- at a higher level
- outside their current reality
- clearly, to create a clear mental picture.

Typically the interviewer would help the interviewee:

- to think through problems
- to consider the organization's goals and its allocation of roles
- to identify learning needs
- to be clear about what action was necessary and about how to take action (with assistance if necessary).

Whatever the formal work system, interviewees were encouraged to consider the natural system and ways to build on it. Often a number of visits were necessary in order to establish a plan which the interviewee felt was his or her own and one which he/she could confidently carry out. The interviewers describe themselves as 'midwives': Grow South! is not in the business of organizing training programmes itself, and its staff are not selling training; rather, they hope to release individuals' motivation to learn and to help them to help themselves in organizing the learning. In their interviews, Grow South! staff acted as interventionists, as (unpaid) external consultants, seeking to provoke the interviewee to identify what he or she already subconsciously knew but had never consciously analysed.

Grow South!'s Researcher is investigating the various 'mind-sets' (the individual's store of beliefs and attitudes) of small business managers in an attempt to classify the differing types. Her work is directed towards enabling the managers to explore their value systems with particular reference to learning (which may or may not be barriers to personal development and hence business growth). She is also looking at ways which enable the small business manager to take the bird's eye view of his or her operation.

In addition to this work, Grow South! is undertaking a large postal survey to:

(i)   reach those who cannot be reached through personal contacts

(ii) to publicize the type of support the project can bring to local firms.

6   Results and achievements

Only an interim report can be given on results; the LCP has another 5 months to run at the time of writing, and even then the extent of Grow South!'s influence will not be easy to measure.

Large organizations' executives have been open with Grow South! staff, not only because the staff seemed already to understand immediate staff development needs (predominantly in the customer care field), but also because they could be regarded as honest and knowledge-able brokers, able to recommend appropriate providers of learning experiences. In some cases, the experience of discussing the organization's learning needs with an outsider proved a cathartic experience for company executives and personnel staff. Wide-ranging discussions on the learning needs of the larger organizations could nonetheless be honed down to arrive at a short list of its real needs. Much of these discussions could therefore focus on ways of meeting needs. As a result of preliminary field work, Grow South! plans to work on a co-ordinated programme for the specialist 'people processing' organizations which are heavily represented in the area.

In the case of interviews with small firms, entrepreneurs were encouraged to formulate their ideas with regard to the organization's goals, the roles of its personnel and, given these, their personal learning needs and the learning needs of staff. The small firms that were visited seemed to be suffering from one or all of three problems: not understanding enough or not being successful enough in the areas of:

  (i)   marketing
 (ii)   accounting
(iii)   interpersonal difficulties between staff – often the two entrepreneurs who owned the business.

Entrepreneurs were able to describe what was 'hurting' in the organization and begin to plan how to overcome the problems they had identified. More than this, they used the opportunity to form a strategic overview of the operation and to set priority tasks and goals. This hypothesis is being tested through further survey data.

A next step for the LCP team has been to encourage networking. That is, to establish links between local organizations in the same line of business for the purpose of pooling experiences and sharing problems from which all participants might learn. Individuals in both large and small organizations have come to understand that the organization's set of learning needs belongs to the day they are determined; clearly it is necessary to continue to monitor learning needs to meet tomorrow's challenges. Networking is seen by the Grow South! team to be an example of true local collaboration and particular emphasis is being given to facilitating the establishment of networks. It is essential for an LCP to set in train some system which can replace it in its role of enthusiasm-generator, focus, and information source. Grow South! staff consider that local networks, which can themselves form a further system of networks, is one answer on the South Bank. Ultimately, Grow South! hopes to establish a 'user-friendly' centre locally where individuals from very small firms can meet to discuss problems and share expertise and thus continue to learn.

An important result of the work so far is the Grow South! team's clear perception that the steps it took in establishing the LCP might be a useful model for the establishment of an LCP anywhere; the steps are replicable and easy to follow (see in particular the section headed 'The Identification of Learning Needs'). It is necessary to set rigorous boundaries if an LCP is to be properly managed and, most importantly, if the client population's real needs are to be met. To this end, the time spent on defining a region and interviewing local employers formed an important precursor to subsequent strategy formulation.

7   Problems

Obviously, real life learning needs are not always easy to label neatly. The Grow South! team has found the simplifying and systematizing of reality problematic. Simply put, the problem is making learning needs intelligible in order that an attempt can be made to achieve them.

Face to face meetings with individuals is a workable way of helping them think about their own and their people's real, job specific and organization specific learning needs, and perhaps even change their attitude to training. It is, of course, an extremely painstaking and time-consuming exercise, very demanding of resources. (The individuals able to conduct such face to face interviews effectively are scarce.)

To do the groundwork necessary to facilitate the establishment of networks will take time, but the work is essential. Grow South! intends to recommend a successor body to carry on the work and to hold a well publicized one-day seminar to bring together people from industry and the support services and to focus both on training and on how the 'patch' functions, adapts to change and learns.

Entrepreneurs running small businesses are likely to be

natural continuous developers: that is, the tasks they find they must perform are of such a range and degree of complexity that they know they must go on learning if their businesses are to survive. (These people have much to teach managers in larger organizations.) Individuals may not be aware of the skills they possess. They need to know where they are now if they are to judge how to get where they want to go next! There is thus a strong case for validating, capturing and recognizing what people do in their jobs, but a good many difficulties in establishing mechanisms for so doing.

8   Next steps

Successful projects develop a momentum all their own. The degree of local support will determine what happens next to Grow South! The (not mutually exclusive) options are:

(1) continuation of Grow South! into a second year

(2) initiation of new LCPs in specific fields (printing, for example)

(3) creation of a small firm support centre

(4) development of Polytechnic services offering short courses and consultancy locally.

Chapter Five
Prompt Lists
Harry Barrington and Sue Wood

Introduction

The three Prompt Lists which follow for:

> Personnel and Training Managers
> Line Management
> Senior Executives

are intended to assist readers to organize their thoughts and begin to draw conclusions with regard to actions. The lists interrelate. Each attempts to help readers to come to terms with what is expected of individual managers according to his or her role, and with what individuals can expect from his or her management partners. Feel free to photocopy the lists and distribute them to and discuss them with your colleagues.

Prompt List for Personnel and Training Managers

This Prompt List offers an opportunity for Personnel and/or Training Managers to explore the 'continuous development' (CD) concept and apply it to their own organizations.

If you are not already well used to CD ideas, you are advised to look first at other chapters in the book, notably Chapters Two and Three.

The Prompt List takes the form of a sequential set of questions. After the first, each answer should be *unique*, addressing your own aims rather than conforming to a set, theoretical ideal. Italicized notes are not meant to offer 'school solutions', but merely to suggest points of consideration for those who want help.

1   **What are the key elements in a 'continuous development' (CD) culture?**

Look at the chapters noted above. The MAIN element is a continuing search for IMPROVED PERFORMANCE. To that end, the CD culture will promote:
  - *continuous learning*
  - *the integration of learning with work*
  - *learning strategies.*

2   **Who should create 'learning strategies'?**

Normally TOP MANAGEMENT – they should create them AS PART OF THEIR OPERATIONAL STRATEGIES. But you may need to help them – for example, by:
  - *suggesting 'improved performance goals'*
  - *reminding them that operational change carries with it learning needs*
  - *proposing improvements to the learning system*
  - *asking that learning strategies are MADE EXPLICIT in forward planning documents*
  - *spelling out specific strategic options.*

3   **What sorts of 'operational change' demand learning strategies?**

ALL SORTS:
  - *technological (new equipment, new materials, new processes)*
  - *legal (new laws, new regulations)*
  - *human (new people)*
  - *organizational (new jobs, new work patterns, new procedures).*

4   **Do we need a special CD system?**

This depends on what you already have, or perhaps on what you have not. (If you don't understand how your organization operates as a learning system, you may need to devise a learning strategy to that end.) You almost certainly need ways of:

- *reviewing performance*
- *identifying learning needs*
- *making learning plans*
- *tapping learning resources.*

These need to be linked to your other operational activities on a continuing basis.

5   Who is responsible for the CD system?

This also depends on your 'normal practice' – or on whatever has been prescribed. But YOU are likely to be the key person. The CD system involves both people and work, but its emphasis on LEARNING usually gives 'custody' to the Personnel and/or Training function.

6   Shouldn't the system itself be developed 'continuously'?

You are unlikely to reach any other decision. A 'strategy for learning' is likely to contain items geared to the system as well as items for developing people. You should try to ensure that any set of forward strategies contains at least one strategy for developing the system.

7   Who creates the actual plans?

This is something to be decided, and indeed to publicize, if it isn't already made clear to all. It need not necessarily be YOU, just because you accept professional responsibility for the system. One much-praised approach makes LINE MANAGEMENT responsible for the plans (and integrating them with other operations) with you responsible for advising them on LEARNING PROCESSES.

8   How do we ensure that the training is 'integrated with work'?

You must work on this to give it practical meaning, using your organization's language and accepting your organization's procedures. BUT it might help you to think about three possible LEVELS of integration by managers:

   a. *dovetailing training activities with other activities on a time basis*

b. *establishing learning OBJECTIVES, and encouraging employees to arrange their work to meet those objectives*

c. *actively demonstrating to others the personal CD style, intervening to make learning happen WHENEVER a problem or an 'improved performance' opportunity is perceived.*

This last level is probably the CD ideal: without creating formal plans, the manager develops operational strength when the need to develop is REAL. At that time there is no distinction between learning and work.

9   How can I find out more?

This is a good example of a learning need, demanding a plan BY YOU, INTEGRATED WITH YOUR WORK and probably SUSTAINED ON A CONTINUING BASIS. You might start by looking at this Prompt List again; then study other chapters in the book, including the case examples and the reading lists; and, finally, you might commit yourself to PRACTISING CD in your own job at your workplace.

Prompt List for Line Management

This Prompt List offers an opportunity for line managers to explore the 'continuous development' (CD) concept and apply it to their own organizations.

If you are not already well used to CD ideas, you are advised to look first at other chapters in the book, notably Chapters Two and Three.

The Prompt List takes the form of a sequential set of questions. After the first, each answer should be *unique*, addressing your own aims rather than conforming to a set, theoretical ideal. Italicized notes are not meant to offer 'school solutions', but merely to suggest points of consideration for those who want help.

1   What are the key elements in a 'continuous development' (CD) management style?

The main element is a never-ending concentration on IMPROVED PERFORMANCE. To that end, a CD style will promote:

- *continuous learning*
- *self development*
- *learning resources*
- *the integration of learning with work.*

2   Am I clear about the main planks in my organization's operational strategy in so far as they affect my areas of responsibility?

Many line managers in many organizations ARE NOT. Your top management should give you any information you need – but you in turn have a responsibility to request it and indeed to discuss it with your superior(s) if you are not clear about its implications. If top management have not formulated an operational strategy, you should press them to create one, and again to keep reviewing and updating it.

3   What is the link between operational strategy and learning strategy?

The latter should be part of the former. If it is not made explicit, you should study all items relating to OPERATIONAL CHANGE:

- *technological (new equipment, new methods, new materials)*
- *legal (new laws or regulations)*
- *human (new people)*
- *organizational (new jobs, new work patterns, new procedures).*

You may need to DEDUCE learning strategy from the aims and priorities; if you can't, you should talk with your superior(s), urging them to influence those who create operational strategy to make learning strategy more explicit.

4   Who should create 'learning strategy'?

Normally top management. But you may need to help them. Your best inputs to them will be:

- *assessing performance on a continuing basis, and ensuring that your superiors get your assessments*
- *suggesting 'improved performance' goals*
- *making sure the learning system works.*

5   What is meant by the 'learning system'?

You need to work on this, to give it a personal meaning. It will probably include those parts of your work system which MAKE LEARNING HAPPEN, including:

- *information on strategic aims*
- *information on current performance*
- *recruitment plans*
- *YOUR OWN DECISIONS ON LEARNING NEEDS AND TRAINING PLANS.*

6   Does this mean that I should create learning plans?

Does the system or strategy require that someone else do this? IF NOT, YOU almost certainly SHOULD. If you aren't certain, then discuss it with your superior(s). But even if someone else IS named, you will surely need to talk through the plans with your subordinates. In some organizations the responsibility is shared, with the aims and content being determined by you, and the training methods by a training specialist or a training supplier.

7   How do I ensure that it is done 'continuously'?

Try building it into your day to day style. You need to be CONTINUOUSLY seeking improved performance opportunities in line with operational aims, and each opportunity should be transformed into a training plan. You should be ready to turn yourself into a learning aid or otherwise call on someone who can provide expertise (as a TEACHER, a TUTOR, a COACH, a COUNSELLOR, a QUESTIONER, a LISTENER, a DECISION

MAKER, and so on) at a moment's notice if that is needed by the plan. Equally you should be ready to turn yourself into a LEARNER if the plan demands learning on your part.

8   I'm still not clear about 'integrating learning with work' How is it done?

Something else you must work on to give it a practical meaning for yourself, using your own language and accepting your own concerns. There are several levels of commitment:

> – *creating training plans, and ensuring that training activities are dovetailed with other work activities*
> – *establishing learning objectives, and encouraging subordinates to arrange their work to meet those objectives*
> – *actively demonstrating a personal CD style, and INTERVENING to make learning happen WHENEVER a problem or an 'improved perform- ance' opportunity strikes you.*

As implied by the note following the previous question, this last level is the CD ideal: in this ideal, and WITH- OUT WAITING FOR FORMAL TRAINING PLANS, you and your colleagues develop your operational strength when the need to develop is REAL. You do not at that time appreciate a distinction between learning and work – the two are the SAME THING.

9   How can I find out more?

This is a good example of a learning need, which demands a plan of YOUR OWN, INTEGRATED WITH WORK and probably SUSTAINED over a period of time. You might start by reading this Prompt List again; then look at chapters in the book including Chapter Six, 'Enhancing your learning skills', the case examples and the reading lists; and, finally, you might commit yourself to PRAC- TISING CD in your own job at your workplace.

Prompt List for Senior Executives

This Prompt List offers an opportunity for Senior Executives to explore the 'continuous development' (CD) concept and apply it to their own organizations.

If you are not already well used to CD ideas, you are advised to look first at other chapters in the book, notably Chapters Two and Three.

The Prompt List takes the form of a sequential set of questions. After the first, each answer should be *unique*, addressing your own aims rather than conforming to a set, theoretical ideal. Italicized notes are not meant to offer 'school solutions', but merely to suggest points of consideration for those who want help.

1   Which items in an operational strategy can be said to be potentially 'continuous development' (CD) items?

All items relating to change:

- *technological (new equipment, new processes)*
- *legal (new laws or regulations)*
- *human (new people)*
- *organizational (new work patterns, new procedures).*

ALL THESE ARE LIKELY TO DEMAND STRATEGIES FOR LEARNING – and ideally your learning strategies will be included as part of your operational strategy for effectiveness.

2   Who creates 'strategies for learning'?

Almost certainly YOU – TOP MANAGEMENT. If you continue with this Prompt List, you can develop your own appreciation of the sorts of things that might be involved in such strategies, and how they might be created.

3   Do we need a special CD system?

This depends on what you already have or have not. (If you don't already understand how your organization operates as a learning system, you may need to devise a strategy to that end.) You almost certainly need ways of:

- *reviewing performance*
- *identifying learning needs*
- *making learning plans*
- *tapping learning resources.*

These need to be linked to your other operational activities on a continuing basis.

4   How do we set about creating 'strategies for learning'?

Here is one possible approach:

a. *you get to know your present 'learning system', especially how your organization creates and implements learning plans*
b. *you establish some learning AIMS or GOALS or PRIORITIES with the requirements of operational change in mind*
c. *you re-develop your learning system in the light of these aims, goals or priorities*
d. *you TELL SUBORDINATES about AIMS, SYSTEM and COMMITMENT.*

5   Shouldn't the system itself be developed 'continuously'?

You are unlikely to reach any other decision. An effective 'strategy for learning' is likely to contain items geared to developing the system as well as items for developing the people. Some CD advocates try to ensure that each set of forward strategic plans contains at least one strategy for developing the system.

6   Can I construct a brief example of a strategy for developing the system?

Here is one example. To improve the identification of learning needs, XYZ organization decided to introduce a continuing flow of data to top management on such things as product changes, capital proposals, quality targets, competitive activity, and so on. Their 'strategy for developing the system' was aimed at ensuring more frequent and better informed setting of priorities; their strategic instrument was a new, early-warning system for top management.

7   Are there ways of ensuring we don't overlook this need to develop the system?

If you think you WILL overlook it, you need YOUR OWN ideas on this built into your strategy. Other organizations have used the following:

- *timing discussions on training to precede and to follow discussions on operational changes*
- *introducing a requirement that any capital proposal MUST be accompanied by a training plan*
- *integrating presentations of 'learning plans' with annual summaries of appraisal statistics.*

8   Can I be more precise on who we should tell about our learning strategies?

This is itself a strategic decision, and can be included in your strategy. But it is likely that ALL MANAGEMENT must know, and equally likely that any LEARNING AIMS must be communicated to ALL WHO ARE TO LEARN.

9   Who should be responsible for training activity?

This is something else you are likely to need in your strategy (it is part of your system). And you will doubtless want ALL subordinates to know where the responsibility lies, so your decisions will need to extend to ways of communicating this particular answer. It is likely to be line management who must carry the responsibility for devising the plans, and for integrating them with other operations; but you may judge that they need help – and if so, you must spell out who will share the responsibility, and how it will be shared.

10   What sort of help might we need?

*This is another strategic decision: it was implied in the last
answer. The strongest option is likely to be the provision
of ADVICE ON LEARNING PROCESSES – to help the
line management with the creation of their plans. You
may want to decide whether such advice should be available internally (eg in the Personnel Department) or
whether it can be 'bought in' on a periodic or part-time
basis. Most CD advocates resist the temptation to let the
advisers take over responsibility for strategy.*

**11   If I want to improve training activity itself, what do I need to
learn about?**

*This is not an easy question to answer. If you have access
to specialist ADVISERS, talk it through with them, and
try to make sure the conclusions are linked to an appreciation of your organization's future knowledge and skill
attitude needs. In general, you are likely to need to learn
more about:*

- *learning processes*
- *group learning*
- *self development.*

*ALL THREE NEED TO BE MANAGED IN THE CD
CULTURE.*

Chapter Six
Enhancing your learning skills –
a note of guidance for managers

Alan Mumford

Introduction

The responsibility for introducing continuous development, and its success, lies with organizations' management teams. In order to promote a new approach to learning, managers need to be knowledgeable about their own learning needs and styles, and sympathetic to the learning-about-learning needs of their peers and subordinates. This chapter is intended to assist managers to refine their understanding of their own learning process.

1   Learning at work

When asked to decribe how they learned to do their jobs, most managers will say they 'learned from experience'. They will generally describe particular responsibilities they have grown used to holding, and then may specify significant experiences, such as completing a challenging project, making an important presentation, or averting a threatened strike. They will usually report a growth in competence and confidence as a result of the experience.

However, it is by no means certain that all managers *will* learn all there is to learn from such experiences. While it is true to say that learning is often a natural, subconscious process, the fact is that learning from experience can be a very inefficient, hit-or-miss operation, and that relying on learning as a natural process is as useful as saying that it is natural for humans to walk. It *is* natural, and perhaps people would learn to walk somehow without any guidance, but guidance helps the process to be both quicker and easier (and to seem more natural more quickly and easily).

Learning from experience is only likely to be effective if it is treated like any other serious management process. Ideally it may mean actually planning the learning experience in advance in order to identify what could be learned from it. Perhaps the manager might have thought about this himself, perhaps in discussion with his own boss. In many cases, however, managers are unlikely to have the opportunity to think beforehand about the kind of learning which might be involved. It is possible, however, for them to think carefully about the experience afterwards.

In either case it is helpful to see learning from experience as involving a cycle:

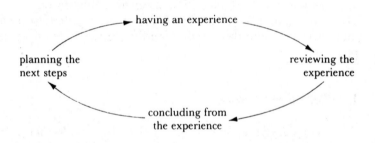

When managers say that they learn from experience, their statement may well be true but partial: that is to say, they have learned, but may not have learned all there was to learn, from the experience. The concern of this chapter is to establish that *learning how to learn* is itself a major managerial requirement, no less important and perhaps even more important than, for example, learning the skills of how to negotiate, how to make decisions and how to understand management accounts. Of course, there are some managers who are not particularly interested in learning anything, but they will not be reading this book.

2   Personal experiences of learning

There will almost certainly be experiences in your own managerial career which you might think to be particularly important. There may also be some experiences which you found to be bad or unhelpful. A useful starting point for considering your own approach to learning is to start from a review of those learning experiences.

Personal experiences of learning – individual task

Look back over your managerial career and identify what you consider to be:

Your two most significant learning experiences. What were the main things you learned, and how did you learn them?

Your two least helpful learning experiences. What might you have learned and what prevented you?

You will probably find it helpful to think back over jobs, tasks and projects in which you have been involved, courses you have attended, books you have read. If you want further hints on the kind of experiences that may have helped or hindered your learning, look ahead in the chapter to the section headed 'Opportunities for learning' (page 178).

It may be that when you have completed this exercise you can compare your results with those of other managers working with you. If you are able to do this, you will probably find that the feature common to most of you is that it is indeed the experience of working on management itself which has provided the most significant learning for you. However, you will probably also find that there are considerable differences in what your colleagues have learned from experiences apparently similar to your own. This phenomenon is encountered particularly with off-the-job courses. Managers with the same learning needs attending the same course at the same time with the same tutors, sometimes emerge at the end with quite different results, one manager apparently having learned a great deal and the other not having learned much at all.

The fact that managers learn differently from the same kind of events ought to explode the myth that most managers are reluctant to learn, or the alternative myth that managers are prepared to learn only from one particular kind of experience. Lazy and inefficient educators and trainers have helped to propagate these myths. Why should anyone be surprised by, or attempt to deny by their practice, the obvious proposition that since people vary in their approach to most aspects of behaviour, they are likely to do so as well in terms of how they respond to particular kinds of learning?

The essential proposition for the individual manager about learning to learn is therefore that he or she *is* individual and that attempts to improve his or her ability as a learner must be based on an understanding by the individual of him or herself.

3   The benefits of learning to learn

Managers who have been helped to learn more effectively will be able to contribute more both to meeting their own needs and the needs of their employers. The benefits of learning to learn at work include:

- an increase in the *capacity* to learn
- an increase in the *motivation* to learn
- development of new learning *opportunities*
- *less dependence* on bosses and teachers
- a multiplier effect – *helping subordinates*
- *confidence* in addressing new challenges.

Managers are motivated to want to learn anything, and certainly to learn how to learn, by a desire to perform more effectively in those core activities which they feel strongly to be the reality of their managerial work.

Therefore, to many practising managers the benefits of learning to learn are that they will be able to learn from experiences, or from courses, more quickly and more effectively.

Learning to learn is a means to an end. It helps managers who:

- have a desire to increase their competence in particular areas
- wish to improve their career prospects
- want to add to their achievements in their current job, or personal satisfaction within it.

It can help reduce frustration and worry caused by ineffective management practices, and even more, by ineffective learning processes.

Perhaps most important of all, in the context of the number of job changes which managers will have, is that learning to learn improves the capacity of managers to adapt to the job changes which they are bound to experience.

The benefits of learning – individual task

Think about a significant management problem which you resolved, concentrating on events in the last year or so. Could you have tackled the problem better or more quickly if you had learned something more effectively earlier in your career?

Think about the same experience and what you have learned from it. List the benefits of learning to learn at work. Have you considered and drawn together all the aspects which might be relevant to carrying out a similar task in the future?

4   Preferred styles of learning

Modern management development practice is just beginning to catch up with the common experience of many managers. If we expose two managers to exactly the same kind of learning experience, we find quite often that one learns and the other does not. Managers who share the results of the individual tasks set so far will probably find from those exercises further evidence to support what many managers in one sense already know. Individuals differ in their willingness and capacity to learn from any particular experience. The learning cycle shown on page 172 is one way of seeing the differences. Some managers are very good at throwing themselves into activities and thereby generating a lot of experience, but much less good at reviewing what they have learned from experience. Some managers are very interested to pick up practical ideas and techniques which they can apply immediately, whereas others are more interested to acquire general ideas and concepts.

One way of describing these differences is to categorize learners under four headings as follows:

ACTIVISTS, WHO LEARN BEST FROM RELATIVELY SHORT, 'HERE AND NOW' TASKS. These may be managerial activities on-the-job or on courses: such things as business games and competitive teamwork exercises. They learn less well from situations involving a passive role such as listening to lectures or reading.

REFLECTORS, WHO LEARN BEST FROM ACTIVITIES WHERE THEY ARE ABLE TO STAND BACK, LISTEN AND OBSERVE. They like collecting information and being given the opportunity to think about it. They learn less well when they are rushed into things without the opportunity to plan.

THEORISTS, WHO LEARN BEST WHEN THEY CAN REVIEW THINGS IN TERMS OF A SYSTEM, A MODEL, CONCEPT OR THEORY. They are interested in and absorb ideas even where they may be distant from current reality. They learn less well from activities presented without this kind of background.

PRAGMATISTS, WHO LEARN WHEN THERE IS AN OBVIOUS LINK BETWEEN THE SUBJECT MATTER AND A PROBLEM OR OPPORTUNITY ON THE JOB. They like being exposed to techniques or processes which can be applied in their immediate circumstances. They learn less well from learning events which seem distant from reality.

Preferred styles of learning – individual task

Do any of the statements listed above seem particularly true or particularly untrue of your own approach to learning?

The statements are very much an *hors d'oeuvre* rather than the full main course. The answers you may have produced will not be fully definitive, but may have excited your interest enough for you to want to pursue the issue further. Ways of doing this are indicated in 'Further Reading', where there will also be found a reference to the work of David Kolb, from whose original ideas this approach derives.

The idea of differences in preferred learning styles is essential to the process of helping managers learn how to learn. At one level it provides improved understanding of the answers managers may have given earlier on previous learning experiences. Managers learn well from activities which are acceptable to them in terms of their learning styles. Those managers who have been taken through the full diagnostic exercise of a Learning Styles Questionnaire (see Honey and Mumford in 'Further Reading'), are able thereafter to make conscious choices about activities in terms of whether they believe themselves likely to learn from them. This would certainly lead to reduced frustration and less wasteful use of time and money. However, at a different level the learning styles approach can be used even more positively. Of course, it is preferable that managers are able to learn from the widest possible variety of learning activities, rather than eliminating some simply because they do not fit existing preferences. It is possible therefore for managers to build up those areas of their preferences which currently cause them to turn away from certain learning processes. This second level approach however is not an easy one. Working through this chapter will certainly help, but attention to the specifics of learning styles needs to be directed through a work book, as suggested in 'Further Reading'.

5 Opportunities for learning

Although managers frequently talk about learning from experience, one of the sadder discoveries from the work which has been done with managers is how limited is their perception of the opportunities available for learning from experience. One of the major features of learning how to learn is therefore simply to extend, to take more advantage of, a wider variety of opportunities to learn. (The following summary of opportunities may also be used in answering the first task set earlier in the chapter (see page 173).)

(a) Changes in jobs and job content.

- promotion to a new job

- job rotation (that is, movement to a job at a similar level but in a different function, product or activity)

- stretching the boundaries of a job by allocating additional responsibilities or tasks

- secondment (that is, movement outside the employing organization to a different job)

- special projects (that is, being given responsibility for a special project outside the normal routines of the current job)

- membership of committees or task groups where normally the content of what was being studied would be within the current experience and competence of the manager involved; sometimes the content could, however, be outside the current job in terms of level or function.

(b) Development processes within the job.

Formal development interventions here include:

- coaching (that is, deliberately taking an individual through problems and issues with the explicit intention of developing his or her understanding and ability to deal with such problems and issues)

- counselling: this would often be done in the context of an appraisal or performance review, and would involve either specific counselling and advice about a particular aspect of performance (or, occasionally, personality), or might involve longer-term career guidance

- mentoring (that is, an activity undertaken by someone other than the manager's direct boss, involving *either* an advisory relationship between a manager and usually a respected senior individual, providing guidance and advice on processes, organizational politics and generally the way to do things, *or* involving a respected senior individual presenting the case for a candidate for a particular job).

(c) Development activities initiated by the individual.

All of the above activities which may be initiated by the organization may in some senses also be sought or pushed for by the individual. There are in addition some activities which the individual is likely to undertake entirely at his or her own initiative.

- modelling on boss, colleagues or outsiders
- reading
- participating in groups of managers from different organizations.

All of these together with planned and integrated off-the-job training might form part of the armoury of any formal management development system in the sense that they could be considered, recommended and applied by advisers, bosses or by individuals themselves. Individual managers are faced with an array of opportunities for self development through every task, every interaction, every problem.

Opportunities for learning – individual task

Which of the opportunities listed above have you personally experienced?

What were the major things you learned from the process?

Do you now see opportunities which you missed by not being aware of the learning possibilities involved?

What made the learning experience helpful and significant to you?

6   Factors influencing learning

So far, we have identified three major influences on how managers learn:

- past experience of learning may have been rewarding or demotivating
- the reality of learning for most managers is that it occurs within the jobs they do rather than outside
- managers differ in their preferred methods of learning.

In fact, managers are subject to an even wider range of influences. Here are some examples:

I worked for a boss who picked out a topic each week to discuss with me: something he had done, something I had done. I learned from the content of the discussion of course – but I also learned how valuable this sort of review could be.

I went on a course involving a lot of video and feedback.

To be really honest I found it difficult to cope with it – it was too public for personal skills.

In my last organization you had to pretend to be fully knowledgeable about everything; it was very risky to suggest you could improve yourself.

Here is a list of the many things which may influence the individual's willingness or ability to learn:

(a) The job environment

 - job content
 - boss
 - colleagues
 - subordinates.

(b) Individual approaches to learning

 - past experience of learning
 - rewards or punishments for learning
 - personal preferences – learning style
 - personal blockages
 - skills for learning.

(c) Learning processes

 - appropriate method
 - teacher/facilitator/coach
 - range of opportunities.

(d) The organizational environment

 - extent to which culture and climate favour learning.

The organizational climate is very important. Whether or not a manager takes the need to learn seriously, and encourages learning through a variety of processes and opportunities, is clearly significant. Changing the organizational climate from a negative or uncaring one in terms of learning is, however, as difficult as it is to change organizational beliefs in any other area. For the purpose of this chapter therefore, the emphasis is on helping the individual manager to understand and deal with those aspects of learning which are within individual control.

Factors influencing learning – individual task

Review your own position on the list of influences given above.

Which do you think are the most powerful for you at present? Were other things more influential in the past?

7   Blockages to learning

Partly because of positive influences around them, some people are in general eager to learn. Some have elements in their personality which encourage them to learn at least in some situations.

However, just as some organizations are uncaring and unsupportive about learning, some managers are held back in their response to opportunities for learning, or in their recognition of opportunities.

I can't see any way in which training could improve that skill.

If I take up that job opportunity, will my current experience be thrown away?

I am much too busy with my job to think about what I'm learning from it.

The following list of blockages to learning, derived from the original work of Temple and Boydell (see 'Further Reading'), helps to explain what holds some individuals back.

Perceptual   – not seeing there is a problem

Cultural   – the organization does not support learning

Emotional   – fear of insecurity

Motivational	– unwillingness to take risks

Cognitive/
Intellectual
	– previous learning experience
	  – limited learning style
	  – poor learning skills

Expressive	– poor communication skills
Situational	– lack of opportunities
Physical	– place, time
Specific environment	– boss/colleagues unsupportive

Blockages to learning – individual task

Consider the list above.

> Which may have restricted your learning in the past?
> Which do you feel may be inhibiting you at the
> moment?

8   Skills of learning

It is possible to identify and work on skills involved in
learning. These can be reviewed under two headings, as
below.

(a) Effective learning behaviour

   (1) Set managerial standards of performance (that is,
      determine what you need to be able to do well)

   (2) Review your achievements against those require-
      ments

   (3) Identify in what areas you need to learn in order
      to perform more effectively

   (4) Identify the opportunities for learning available
      to you (see the list earlier in this paper)

   (5) Analyse influences, blockages and learning styles
      (see earlier exercises)

    (6) Develop a personal learning plan.

(b) Crucial learning skills

    (1) Listening

    (2) Taking risks

    (3) Sharing

    (4) Accepting help

    (5) Monitoring achievement.

Skills of learning – individual task

How good am I at each of the items mentioned above?

Look again at the list of opportunities you reviewed on pages 178–80. Which skills do you need to develop further to achieve the goals you set for yourself there?

Who might help me, first in reviewing how good I am and secondly in helping me to improve both the learning skills and the managerial skills I want to develop?

9   A learning log

One of the best ways of relating learning to the normal reality of managerial experience is to keep a learning diary or log. This does not imply something with the same amount of detail as Pepys. It could sensibly involve keeping perhaps a daily but certainly a weekly log of significant managerial events in your life. It could mean, for example, recording the main things you learn from attending a meeting or managing a major project. The log or diary, therefore, could be entirely something written in hindsight, related to particular activities. The hindsight might be directed to an earlier plan, so that for example a manager who developed some ideas as a consequence of this section on *learning skills* could use the log to monitor what had actually happened on them.

Some managers have gone further and made the log into both a hindsight document and a continuous working plan. They have used it to identify opportunities which might be coming up, to reflect on needs which derived from current managerial activities and to make statements about what they were going to do about them.

Not all managers would find the learning log process a comfortable one. Some of you will immediately have spotted that it is a process which is more natural to the *reflector* learning style than it is to the *activist* learning style. For *activists* it is, however, a process which could be particularly helpful, if they decided they wanted to extend the range of their learning styles.

One of the most valuable aspects of a learning log can be that it helps managers to review learning from many different points of view. As a consequence it helps them to integrate their activities. It helps them see how a managerial activity is also a learning opportunity. It helps them analyse how well they have taken advantage of that opportunity. It helps them identify additional learning needs, and the identification of additional or improved learning skills.

10   Definitions of learning to learn

The structure of this paper will, so far, probably have been more satisfactory to *pragmatists* and *reflectors* than to *theorists*.

Learning to learn – individual task

Consider why the above statement is true as a general proposition. Has it been true for you as an individual?

It is sensible if, in terms of the purposes of the paper and of the needs of *theorists*, we conclude with some statements about the basic concept of learning from which the paper is derived. You have already been exposed to the model of learning from experience as a circular process (page 172).

To that model we can now add some statements about the motivations for, and content of, the learning process:

- Our earlier experience at school and perhaps university is one of being taught, of being given instruction by an authoritative figure on a discrete subject in a scholastic environment

- Managers are in fact rarely exposed to the equivalent process, and are often inclined to reject it in whole or in part even when offered

- Managers are most inclined to respect as relevant learning processes which build on the experiences of themselves and others

- It is the nature of managerial jobs that they provide a rich diversity of experience, and that real learning is equated with effectively undertaking managerial tasks rather than analysing or theorizing about how such tasks might be undertaken

- Effective learning occurs when relevance is combined with realistic learning processes attached to the ability of the individual manager to learn from that process.

This chapter is designed to show the four major elements of learning to learn:

- Helping managers to know the stages of the learning process, and blockages to learning

- Helping them to understand their own preferred approaches to learning

- Assisting managers in making best use of their existing learning preferences, or building additional strengths and overcoming blockages

- Helping managers to carry their understanding of learning from off-the-job to on-the-job opportunities.

It will be noted that the emphasis throughout the chapter has been on enabling managers to learn in a variety of situations. This emphasis is necessary not only because structured learning experiences off-the-job will be relatively infrequent for most managers, nor simply because so many opportunities exist that are underused on the job. The point also is to provide a connection between different kinds of learning experience, and to enable managers to continue their learning as they face different challenges and different opportunities throughout their managerial lives.

References and Further Reading

Introduction

Its authors intend that this book should stand alone. Material included in Chapters Two and Six, however, may lead some readers to seek further information. In Chapter Two, a special section was included for the use of IPM (and other) students. The references indicated by bracketed numbers in that section are set out below in List A. Chapter Six will, we hope, have whetted readers' appetites for more information on the subjects of learning how to learn and individual learning styles. References, which follow the sequence of the chapter, follow in List B below.

List A

Since the literature on what and how managers learn in the organizational context is extensive, the following is a selective list of readable books and reports which summarize the extensive research findings.

(1) MANT Alistair. *The experienced manager.* London, British Institute of Management, 1969. 48pp
See also
BRITISH INSTITUTE OF MANAGEMENT and INSTITUTION OF INDUSTRIAL MANAGERS. *Front-line management: a joint BIM/IIM Report.* Corby, BIM and Luton, IIM, 1985. 25pp

(2) MANPOWER SERVICES COMMISSION. *A policy for management development*, Manpower Services Commission, 1980

(3) REVANS Reginald W. *The ABC of action learning.* 2nd ed. Bromley, Chartwell-Brott, 1983. 84pp, charts
See also
REVANS Reginald W. *The origins and growth of action learning.* Bromley, Chartwell-Brott, 1982. xi, 846pp, tables

(4) SINGER Edwin J. *Effective management coaching.* 2nd ed. London, Institute of Personnel Management, 1979. xi, 212pp
See also
MANPOWER SERVICES COMMISSION. Training of Trainers' Advisory Group. *Learn how to learn.* Sheffield, Manpower Services Commission.
See also
LATHROPE K. 'Stop your workforce standing still'. *Personnel Management.* Vol 17, No 10, October 1985. pp 50–53

(5) KOLB David A. *Experiential learning: experience as the source of learning and development.* Englewood Cliffs, N J, Prentice-Hall, 1984. xiii, 256pp
See also
BARRINGTON Harry A. *Learning about management.* Maidenhead, McGraw-Hill, 1984. ix, 235pp
See also
JOHNSON Ron M. *Building success through people.* London, Business Books, 1986.
See also
HONEY Peter and MUMFORD Alan. *Manual of learning styles.* 2nd ed. Maidenhead, Peter Honey, 1986.

(6) BOYDELL Tom and PEDLER Mike. *Management self-development: concepts and practices.* Farnborough, Hants, Gower Press, 1981. xv, 254pp
See also
PEDLER Mike and others. *Self-development groups for*

managers. Sheffield, Manpower Services Commission, 1984. 60pp
See also
PEDLER Mike, BURGOYNE John G *and* BOYDELL Tom. *A manager's guide to self-development.* 2nd ed. London, McGraw-Hill, 1986. v, 236pp

(7)   HANDY Charles. *Understanding organizations.* 2nd ed. Harmondsworth, Middx., Penguin, 1981. 473pp
See also
WILDSMITH J R. *Managerial theories of the firm.* London, Martin Robertson, 1973. 140pp

List B

The idea of learning from experience, particularly on the job, is discussed fully by Mumford (MUMFORD A, *Making experience pay.* Maidenhead, McGraw-Hill, 1980) with a wide range of illustrations.

The original concepts of the learning cycle and individual differences in preferred approaches to learning was developed by David Kolb. While his book (KOLB D. *Experiential learning.* Englewood Cliffs, New Jersey, Prentice-Hall, 1984) would perhaps be of major interest only to those managers interested in the theory of learning, he has produced a Learning Styles Inventory and a Personal Learning Guide specifically directed to a wider audience (KOLB D. *Learning styles inventory.* Boston, Mass., McBer Company, 1985), (KOLB D. *Personal learning guide.* Boston, Mass., McBer Company, 1982).

Honey and Mumford produced their own detailed statement of Learning Styles originally for management developers, trainers and educators (HONEY P and MUMFORD A. *Manual of learning styles.* 2nd ed. Maidenhead, Peter Honey, 1986). This was extended to a booklet (HONEY and MUMFORD. *Using your learning styles.* 2nd ed. Maidenhead, Peter Honey, 1986) specifically directed at managers. It takes them through the marking of results on the Learning Styles Questionnaire, and then shows how managers may use these results either to select activities or to build their less developed learning styles.

Managers who want to see how ideas about learning styles can be incorporated into programmes directed at managerial problem-solving should read Scriven (SCRIVEN R. 'Learning circles'. *Journal of European Industrial Training*. Vol 8, No 1, 1982).

The material indicated so far has been directed at the interests of managers themselves. Management developers, trainers or educators who may also read this book could benefit from a more detailed range of materials.

The only major review of Learning to Learn so far has been that of Mumford who has published both a review of practice (MUMFORD A. 'Learning for managers'. *Journal of European Industrial Training*. Vol 10, No 2, 1986) and a review of the literature (MUMFORD A. 'Learning to learn for managers: a literature review'. *Management Bibliographies and Reviews*. Vol 12, No 2, 1986).

The work of Temporal and Boydell on blockages is to be found in TEMPORAL P and BOYDELL T. *Helping managers to learn*. Sheffield City Polytechnic, 1981.

An extended use of Kolb's LSI and the Learning Cycle in a problem-solving context is given by Richardson and Bennett (RICHARDSON J and BENNETT B. 'Applying learning techniques'. *Journal of European Industrial Training*, Vol 8, Nos 1, 3 and 4, 1984).

Stuart (STUART R. *Maximising managers' day to day learning*, edited by COX C and BECK J. New York, Dave Whiley, 1984) has drawn together Kolb and the work on blockages, and has also made a major contribution in his article on using others to learn (STUART R. 'Using others to learn' in MUMFORD A. *Handbook of management development*. Aldershot, Gower, 1986). Not only does it extend our knowledge in a relatively unstudied area, but it has the major advantage of being centred on normal, everyday experiences.

Honey (HONEY P. 'Styles of learning' in MUMFORD A. *Handbook of management development*. Aldershot, Gower, 1986) is one of the few people to have written about the use of a Learning Log, trebly interesting because it is focused on his own Learning Styles Questionnaire and his own development.

A complete resource on Learning to Learn has been produced (*The learning to learn resource*, 62 Toller Lane, Bradford,

W Yorkshire BD8 9BY, MCB University Press). This includes many of the materials mentioned above and is designed to equip the Management Developer to design and run effective learning to learn experiences.